BORN ONLY ONCE

Other Bks. Feeling and Healing your
Emotions - Conrad W. Baars

Healing the Unaffirmed
by Baars & Terruwe

Psychic Wholeness and
Healing - Terruwe & Baars

BORN ONLY ONCE
The Miracle of Affirmation

Conrad W. Baars, M.D.

Illustrated by William Dichtl

FRANCISCAN HERALD PRESS
1434 WEST 51st STREET • CHICAGO, 60609

Born Only Once by Conrad W. Baars, M.D., copyright
© 1975, Franciscan Herald Press, 1434 West 51st St., Chicago, Illinois 60609.

Library of Congress Cataloging in Publication Data:

Baars, Conrad W.
  Born only once.

  Bibliography: p.
  1. Self-actualization (Psychology) I. Title.
BF637.S4B3   616.8'914   75-23226
ISBN 0-8199-0700-6 (Hard cover)
ISBN 0-8199-0671-9 (Paperback)

First Paperback Edition

Sixth Printing

PRINTED IN THE UNITED STATES OF AMERICA

Dedication

*This book is dedicated
to each person
who feels*

*unloved
unwanted
lonely
unable to make friends
and
to relate to others*

who feels inferior
inadequate
insecure
uncertain of himself
without identity

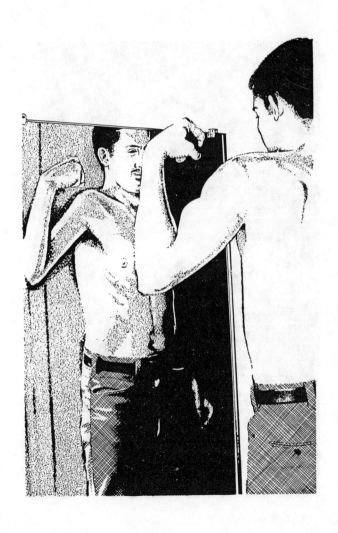

This book is dedicated
to each person
who feels

insignificant and
worthless
like a child
at the mercy of grown-ups
afraid to assert himself
afraid of the world

who feels depressed
and wishes he were dead
or contemplates suicide
or has attempted suicide

who always feels tired
and whose pains and aches
or psychosomatic illness
do not respond adequately
to treatment

This book is dedicated to
the millions of people who
never find true happiness and joy,
even though not *mentally ill,*
nor suffering from any of the neuroses
discovered by Sigmund Freud to be
due to repression of
emotions and feelings

. . . . . and in spite of

a successful career
riches
fame
power over others
a life of doing for others
or of abandonment to sensuality, sexuality.

This book is dedicated to the millions
who have been deprived of their second birth

—their psychic birth—

by a significant, affirming others—
parents, relatives, teachers or friends—
and therefore,
because of circumstances beyond their control
have been deprived of the joy of

AFFIRMATION

Note: In this book "un-affirmed" or "non-affirmed" stands for totally not, partially, or inadequately affirmed. "affirmed" means totally, fairly adequately, or largely affirmed.

CONTENTS

The Miracle of Affirmation

Chapter I

ARE YOU AN AFFIRMED PERSON?

Dear Doctor,

"I feel very depressed and lonely. I am afraid to be with people. I care to talk only to one individual at a time and then only when I think he or she will understand me. Everybody has always said that I am a good priest, but I feel I can't be a priest anymore. I feel like a helpless child and don't know where to turn for help. I am confused and filled with hostilities like a teenager. I am afraid, though, of acting like one because of what I might do and for fear of what people might think of me. I don't feel that anybody understands me, not even my psychiatrist. He advised me to take a leave of absence from the active ministry, and to get a job in order to work on my "self-image." But how can I help myself? I feel devoid of any inner strength. I am exhausted and depleted of all strength I may ever have had.

Can you help me?"

This letter, one of hundreds received during my years in private psychiatric practice, is typical of the way unaffirmed people feel.

A woman from Missouri was only half way through the chapter, "The Frustration Neurosis" in *Loving and Curing the Neurotic*[1] when she wrote me,

"I felt that you had to be inside me somehow, or picked my brain before you wrote that chapter. The things you say your patients relate to you are the very same things I have said to someone I have been able to trust. Five or six years ago I wrote the following:

> '*They expected me to be a little girl—*
> *I was never a baby.*
> *They expected me to be a teen-ager—*
> *I was never a little girl*
> *They expected me to be a woman—*
> *I was never a teen-ager.*
> *They expected me to be a wife—*
> *I was never a woman.*
> *They expected me to be a mother—*
> *I was never a wife.*
>
> *——I was never born!*' "

And a third person, already in treatment, expressed

---

1. Anna A. Terruwe, M.D. and Conrad W. Baars, M.D. (New Rochelle, New York: Arlington House Publishers, 1972) An abridged, revised paperback edition will be published in 1976 under the title, *Healing the Unaffirmed*, Alba House, Staten Island, N.Y.

in poetic language her isolation and loneliness, her sense of abandonment, and search for identity:[2]

> *"Lord, where they live, I cannot stay*
> *and where I live, their world comes to an*
> * end;*
> *a little blossom only makes me feel so sad,*
> *Smaller than ever seems my chance to be*
> * myself.*
>
> *First they excluded me from the children*
> * they'd planned,*
> *now their mind cleaves the time and grasps*
> * for power,*
> *early they learned to ban a stranger from*
> * their land,*
> *When bedtime comes I kiss myself goodnight*
>
> *And endless suffering is softly whispered in*
> * my ear*
> *I take it in the hollow of my hand . . .*
> *And I protest, oh Lord, against so many*
> * murders,*
>
> *Why do I have to die in my own words*
> *And why must I be chained to my own*
> * being . . .*
> *who shall I be, Lord, in Your promised*
> * Land?"*

---

2. Ibid. p. 332.

DEPRIVATION

These three unaffirmed persons speak eloquently of their intense sufferings and unhappiness. Each in his own way describes some of the symptoms of an emotional illness which in its most severe form is called frustration, or deprivation neurosis. It is *the* neurosis of our times, *the* cause of infinitely varied misery and unhappiness. Its incidence in the Western World is growing by leaps and bounds.

However, there are even many, many more people who manifest the same, though much less intense symptoms without being in need of psychiatric treatment. Their suffering, although essentially the same as that of persons with a full blown deprivation neurosis, is less disabling, less crippling and therefore allows more room for attempts at counteracting and coping with it.

To what extent a person will become affected will depend on the age at which a person began to be deprived of affirmation, and to what extent, and by whom. But whether severely affected or only to a moderate degree, the consequences of being deprived of affirmation in early life affect our entire society at all levels and in a great variety of ways—from alienation to zero population growth. The condition feeds on itself.

Deprivation neurotic parents rear deprivation neurotic children; deprivation neurotic people create polarization with all its dire consequences for families, communities, countries and the world.

It is time that this condition be universally recognized by psychiatrists, physicians, psychologists, counselors, clergy and religious of all faiths, educators, politicians and rulers of nations.

MAN IN THE STREET

But, most importantly, it should be recognized by the man in the street, the common man with common sense, who ordinarily determines the ultimate fate of a nation, and in our times, of the world. The common man, even more than the professionals, can do much to stop this self- and other-defeating process of non-affirmation, to affirm those already afflicted, and to prevent its development in future generations.

Therefore, in order that all of us can determine to what extent we have been affirmed and can help each other, let me describe briefly the syndrome of the unaffirmed individual in its most severe form—the frustration or deprivation neurosis:[3]

1) An inability to relate to others, to form intimate friendships or a truly loving marital relationship.

The deprivation neurotic person feels like a child who is, or feels he is, neither accepted nor understood by other adults. He fears the adult world he must live in. He is only happy when others make the first—and subsequent—steps in relating to him.

---

3. For a complete and detailed description the reader is referred to *Loving and Curing the Neurotic* and *Healing the Unaffirmed*.

2) Feelings of uncertainty and insecurity.

Often the deprivation neurotic cannot make decisions in personal matters. However, in matters which are strictly of a business nature he usually is not handicapped in this way. A deprivation neurotic is usually overly sensitive to the opinions of others, easily hurt by equivocal remarks and slights, often to the point of feeling that people are against him. His excessive desire to please others and his fear of hurting their feelings characterize his non-assertive behavior with other people. He experiences an extreme need for the approval of his actions by significant others.

3) Feelings of inferiority and inadequacy.

Since their feelings of uncertainty cause deprivation neurotics to fail often in whatever they undertake, they develop a sense of being inferior. This manifests itself frequently, particularly in girls, in a feeling that nobody loves them and that nobody could possibly love them. The fact that they did not receive love when they were young is later interpreted to mean that they are not worth loving.

In boys the feeling of inferiority frequently manifests itself as a concern over inadequate virility and masculine physique. Some young men with a deprivation neurosis may mention feelings of inadequacy with regard to their penis because, in their opinion, it is either too small or too large.

In men as well as in women, strong feelings of inferiority also occur in relation to intellectual capacity. Students of superior intelligence, but with a deprivation neurosis, are often convinced that they will never succeed in their studies, or that they have failed in their examinations. Others with superior intelligence or artistic and skillful with their hands never complete their studies or work. When they have begun something they give up after a while with the excuse that they "would not be able to finish it, anyway!"

At times these feelings of inferiority and inadequacy give rise to a deep-seated *feeling of guilt*. This happens when these persons have arrived, intellectually at least, at the level of moral behavior, and they attach to their inadequacies an ethical significance which these acts do not possess at all. They see their inability as a fault to be imputed to the will. They consider themselves evil, devoid of love, without religious feeling, selfish, seeking only themselves, so that as far as they are concerned, every act of theirs cannot but confirm their guilt.

Fortunately, not all deprivation neurotics develop these feelings of guilt, for in many they can be very difficult to modify, based as they are on a deep-rooted, virtually ingrained judgment of their own personality.

Deprivation neurotics with intractable guilt feelings are advised to meditate often on the words of Dr. Carl Jung addressed to the psychotherapist concerning his need to see and accept himself as he is, before he can accept his patients as they are:

"To accept oneself as one is may sound like a simple thing, but simple things are always the most difficult things to do. In actual life to be simple and straightforward is an art in itself requiring the greatest discipline, while the question of self-acceptance lies at the root of the moral problem and at the heart of a whole philosophy of life.

Is there ever a doubt in my mind that it is virtuous for me to give alms to the beggar, to forgive him who offends me, yes, even to love my enemy in the name of Christ? No, not once does such a doubt cross my mind, certain as I am that what I have done unto the least of my brethren, I have done unto Christ.

But what if I should discover that the least of all brethren, the poorest of all beggars, the most insolent of all offenders, yes even the very enemy himself—that these live within me, that I myself stand in need of the alms of my own kindness, that I am to myself the enemy who is to be loved— what then?

Then the whole Christian truth is turned upside down; then there is no longer any question of love and patience, then we say "Raca" to the brother within us; then we condemn and rage against ourselves! For sure, we hide this attitude from the outside world, but this does not alter the fact that we refuse to receive the least among the lowly in ourselves with open arms. And if it had been Christ himself to appear within ourselves in such a contemptible form, we would have denied him a thousand times before the cock had crowed even once!"

4) Increasing feelings of depression.

The deprivation neurotic's fearful non-assertive way of living increases his loneliness. He has neither intimate friends nor strong enemies. He is helpless when others try to take advantage of him, and therefore frequently the victim of the selfishness of others. In time his life becomes so unpleasant and painful that death often seems the only way out. The depth of the depression, the strong possibility of suicide, the sometimes profound feelings of guilt and the despair and loneliness of these persons usually requires psychiatric treatment. But unless the psychiatrist is fully acquainted with the syndrome of the deprivation neurotic and is himself a warm and consistently affirming person, the use of drugs, electroshock treatment, psychoanalysis, etc. is at best palliative. In deprivation neurotics none of these forms of therapy, if devoid of affirmation, can ever effect a cure. In fact, electroshock treatment should virtually always be considered a contraindication in depressed deprivation neurotics. Only authentic affirmation can help these utterly unhappy persons to grow into mature, self-respecting, fulfilled, happy human beings whose healthy love of self will flow over into love of others and of God. [4]

_____

4. When the syndromes of non-affirmation and deprivation neurosis are clearly recognized by the psychiatric profession and the man in the street, the following quotes I believe will become largely obsolete. "A further complication to recognizing depression is that doctors themselves can't agree on what depression is or what causes

Biological birth is not enough. *Psychic birth* through authentic affirmation is an absolute necessity for man to be capable of finding true human happiness in this life. The not-yet affirmed need it: infants and children and deprivation neurotics. The not-yet completely affirmed need it: adolescents and young adults. And the mature adult, too, needs the words of affirmation. Affirmation is at the root of all happy human existence.

---

it. 'It's many different diseases all thrown into one waste-basket,' says Harvard psychiatrist Dr. Joseph Schildkraut. The problem, he says, is that no one has yet been able to identify these diseases.''. . . . . ''Depression is a disease that paralyzes the will and saps the energy and commonly drives people to suicide.'' (Wall Street Journal, April 7, 1972)

It is the depression that first appears as a symptom in the non-affirmed individual, then becomes so intense in the deprivation neurotic that it is seen and experienced as a disease, that accounts in my opinion for the truth of the observation by Dr. Gerald Klerman, Professor of psychiatry at Harvard, ''If the 1950's were the age of anxiety, then the 1970's are the age of melancholy!'' That the situation has not improved noticeably since 1972 is obvious from the following excerpts from an April 7, 1975 article in the Wall Street Journal by Benjamin Stein. ''Almost everyone is interested in mental health, or worried about it. And almost everyone likes to watch television. So a series on television about mental health should be a natural. WNET, the New York educational-public television station, with a grant from the Bristol-Myers Co, made a series of five shows entitled, 'The Thin Edge'. . . . . In the New York City area alone, after the first episode 'Depression - The Shadowed Valley,' there were an estimated 150,000 calls to the station. . . . . Not only that, but the show drew a huge audience for public television - estimated at over 400,000 in New York City alone! . . . . The public's desire for help and knowledge in this area is obviously present!''

Chapter II

WHAT IS AFFIRMATION?

Long ago a friend told me of a childhood incident that had left a lasting impression on him.

He was five or six years old when on a weekday morning the pastor came to visit his mother. His father was outside working on the farm. The older children were in school. Being shy, my friend John hid under the table, but not entirely out of sight, while the pastor and his mother visited. Neither one paid attention to him. When the pastor had left and John had come out from under the table his mother stroked his hair and with a friendly smile said, "Were you shy, Johnny"?

Johnny had never forgotten this incident and the wonderful feeling that it was all right for him to be shy, that he did not have to force himself to be a big boy and to hide his shyness from the visitor.

Johnny had been affirmed both by his mother and her understanding visitor. They had affirmed Johnny by allowing him to grow and become who and what he was supposed to be in his own time, in his own way, and at his own pace.

I remember asking John whether he recalled the effect of this particular visit. "Indeed", he replied, "I remember that it gave me a sense of confidence in myself, a feeling that I was O.K. And I'm almost positive that the visit cured, or at least greatly diminished my shyness".

This may sound like a rather unexpected outcome to those of us who find it easier to imagine another version of this visit by the pastor, like "Johnny, come out from under the table and shake hands with the pastor. Show him what a big boy you are. Come on, Johnny, don't be a baby." But it is precisely the Johnny in this second version who is not being affirmed and whose emotional development will become adversely affected.

So is little Mary not affirmed who throws a temper tantrum and gets a spanking for doing so from her mother (and for scaring her by turning blue in the face!)

So is Jimmy not affirmed, when he comes home angry and crying after getting hurt in a fight with another boy in front of his house, and is told by his father, "You sissy, go after him and get even with him. No son of mine is going to let himself be beaten up by anybody"!

An affirming parent, who finds delight in and accepts his child precisely the way he is at that moment, and is not driven by a need or desire to hurry his development or to correct any existing faults or shortcomings: such a parent would have treated Jimmy differently. He would have put his arm around the angry Jimmy and let him cry. And when Jimmy had calmed down, he might have said, "Does it hurt, Jimmy?" or, "Are you sad, Jimmy?" or "Do you want to tell me about it"?

By this tender acceptance of Jimmy in his grief and pain, the affirming parent discloses to him that he finds delight in Jimmy as he is—sad or happy— because he is Jimmy. And it is exactly and solely this tender, almost non-verbal disclosure of Jimmy's goodness and lovableness that is perfectly attuned to Jimmy's level of development, to his capacity of receiving it and responding to it.

AFFIRMATION IS BEING, NOT DOING

Contrary to what many people think, there is little actual doing involved in affirmation. Authentic affirmation is first of all a state of being. Only secondarily may it lead to doing, to acts, to words, that may then complete the affirmation of the other. But they do not constitute the essence, the core of the affirming process. To explain this more precisely is one of the reasons why I decided to write this book. For there is much pseudo-affirmation being practiced nowadays, and not enough authentic affirmation especially in various modern therapeutic and counseling situations.

Some of the other reasons for writing this book are:

1) There is so little real joy and happiness in the world.
2) So much unhappiness is man-made.

3) So few people know how to love and make others happy.
4) There is so much selfishness in the world.
5) The number of unaffirmed people to whom this book is dedicated is so very large and growing all the time at an alarming rate.
6) Even the psychiatric profession seems to be in the dark by and large about the nature of the deprivation neurosis, about "this new kind of neurotic caseload . . . . with a heterogeneous stew of psychological, social, moral and existential ingredients (loneliness, despair, unhappiness, lack of fulfillment, and uncertainty in one's sense of personal identity.) . . . for whom exploratory psychotherapy does not seem to work very well . . . since for these patients the unconscious seems to have lost a good deal of its mysterious and noxious quality."[1]

Affirmation, I said before, is not primarily a matter of doing something to another, but a state of being. This may be a discouraging remark if you expected this to be a *"how-to-do-it"* book, especially if you had bought this book in order to do something special for someone you care about. But do not lose courage, you need only to do less and to be more, for your own sake as well as that of others.

---

1. "Changing Styles in the Neuroses" by Paul Chodoff, M.D., read at the 1972 Annual Convention of the American Psychiatric Association.

If you are already sufficiently affirmed this book can only put in words what you already are to yourself and to others. It will give you insight into how you have been—spontaneously and naturally—

a source of affirmation and therefore of happiness to others. Thus is could facilitate your helping others to be the same. You will also be able to understand why many people have become their own worst enemies trying to find happiness through self-affirmation[2]. You may have opportunities to do something for self-affirming persons you know, either on an individual basis, or even on a larger scale.

If, on the other hand, you are one of the many to whom I have dedicated this book, you will learn how you can become open to being affirmed by others, open to your second or psychic birth. This second birth will open the door of your lonely prison cell and enable you, however belatedly, to find joy in all the good within and around you.

BEING OPEN

In order to become open to all existing goodness, and thus to find happiness through affirming that goodness, whether in beings or in things, you first have *to be you*. In order to be you, you must first *become you*. In order to become you, you must first *receive* the gift of yourself. In order to receive this gift, there has to be another who *gives*, who gives without taking, without demanding anything, who gives you what is not his own, but yours, your own goodness. The other can do this only when he is already happy with himself, and thus

---

2. See Chapter V.

open to the goodness of all else.

In a certain sense, therefore, this is a *how-to-be* book, or, if you will, a *how-to-become* book. You will learn how not to do so much, and thus break the vicious circle of being frustrated and unhappy in this futile effort to make yourself happy. This reminds me of the unfortunate choice o° words at the end of the beautiful verse, *Desiderata,*[3]

> *Beyond a wholesome discipline, be gentle with yourself. You are a child of the universe, no less than the trees and the stars; you have a right to be here. And whether or not it is clear to you, no doubt the universe is unfolding as it should.*
>
> *Therefore be at peace with God, whatever you conceive Him to be, and whatever your labors and aspirations, in the noisy confusion of life keep peace with your soul.*
>
> *With all its sham, drudgery and broken dreams, it is still a beautiful world.*
>
> *Be careful. Strive to be happy.*

It is like saying, "be careful—breathe." Why? Because our willing to be happy is as much a

---

3. Max Ehrmann (Boston, Mass: Crescendo Publishing Co., 1927).

natural, spontaneous, involuntary process as breathing. Man is as unfree in choosing to be unhappy as he is unfree in choosing not to breathe. The great theologian, Thomas Aquinas expressed this succinctly seven hundred years ago in the words, "happiness is what the will is incapable of not willing," and somewhere else he wrote "man strives for happiness naturally and by necessity." Therefore any excessive striving for happiness is just as unhealthy as are any excessive efforts at breathing. Through excessively fast breathing we develop hyperventilation accompanied by cramps and fainting. Through excessive striving for happiness we close ourselves off from the happiness another is ready to give us.

You will agree with me that the author of *Desiderata* said some very beautiful things about being happy, but little about the fundamental process of how to become happy. So let me continue to explain the process of affirmation.

THE PROCESS OF AFFIRMATION

It is an undisputed fact that all human beings desire happiness. Happiness is what we are created for. However, every human being, no matter how many close friends he has is also, in the ultimate analysis, *unique* and *alone*. He stands alone in his unique self, either weakly, inadequately and unhappily; or firmly, strongly and happily. If he perceives himself to be good, worthwhile, desirable, lovable, he will possess himself strongly and firmly. For this sense of one's own *firm*-ness each human

being is totally dependent on another human being's gift of af-*firm*-ation. The earlier in life he receives this gift the sooner his growing firmness and strength enable him to cope with the world, to contribute to the world his own strength, and share his happiness with others.

Your affirmation, your feeling firm and strong, your possessing yourself in joy, your feeling worthwhile, starts with and is dependent on another human being, who:

1) *is aware of, attentive and present to* your unique goodness and worth, separate from and prior to any good and worthwhile thing you may do or can do, and
2) *is moved by, feels attracted to, finds delight in* your goodness and worth, but without desiring to possess you, or use you, or change you, and
3) permits his being moved by and attracted to you *to be revealed* simply and primarily by the psychomotor reactions—visible, sensible physical changes—which are part of his "being moved".[4]

These changes constitute the tenderness and delight revealed in his eyes, his gaze, his touch, his tone of voice and choice of words. They cause you to *feel,* sense, see and hear that you are good and worthwhile—good for the other and good in and for yourself. You come to feel and know who and what you are.[5]

---

4. Many people are emotionally repressed even to the point of suppressing these external signs of their feelings and emotions.

5. How important it is to *feel* as well as *know*, is evident from the observation that even when an unaffirmed person derives satisfaction from his being worthwhile as a *do-er*, and possesses the knowledge that every person, including himself, is worthwhile as a human being, he will still feel lonely and unhappy. Unless someone gives him — through affirmation—the feeling of being worthwhile as a *be-er*, he will remain unhappy for the rest of his life.

Awareness, being moved, and revealing constitute the essence of affirmation. Anything more—helpful deeds, words of advice, gifts, acts of kindness or support, silence, patient waiting, and so on—is the concrete expression of affirmation, but not its essence. Affirmation is first of all *affectivity,* a matter of *feeling.* Only secondarily is it *effectivity,* a matter of *doing.* If the matter of revealing as a *being* process, rather than a *doing* process puzzles you, let me tell you what I learned from Mary, Sally, Helen and others in my psychiatric practice.

At a very early age, Sally, to take one of these patients, had pushed her mother away either when fed or simply when being held. She had been so young at that time that she had no personal recollection of this incident—she had been told this later by her mother, who, judging by my own personal observation, was a typical unaffirmed and possessive woman. She had reacted to her being pushed away by Sally with a feeling of rejection and a subsequent refusal to be a "loving mother" to Sally. From the story of Sally and the others I learned that a very young baby is able to literally *feel* the difference between being loved unselfishly, for his own goodness, and being loved possessively, for the sake of gratifying his mother's need. A baby can sense this only from the visible and sensible physical changes that are part and parcel of every human situation. Judging from the story of Sally these changes differ when the emotion of love is mature, other-directed, and affirming as compared with that which is immature, self-seeking and non-affirming.

AFFIRMATION—A GIFT

Affirmation is a gift freely given with no strings attached. It would be futile to beg for it, demand it, strive for it, endeavor to buy it, or obtain it under false pretenses. If you did not receive it as a child, you can only desire it, hope for it, be open to it, wait for someone to come along who discerns your goodness and worth, and tenderly gives it to you.

> *"I adjure you, daughters of Jerusalem, . . .*
> *do not arouse, do not stir up love before*
> *its own time" (The Song of Songs by*
> *Solomon).*

Once more, I affirm another when I recognize that he is good, worthwhile and lovable, precisely the way he is—period, without the usual addition of "in spite of his shortcomings," since that implies that my recognition and feeling of his goodness is conditional and that he must *do* something. And it is in and through the process of my being aware of, and my feeling of, his goodness that I disclose the other to himself: *"You are good, the way you are; this is the way you may be; there is nobody like you; you are unique!"*

I do not add as is so often done, "I want to help you to become better," since that focuses on his not yet being better and creates in him a sense of being expected to do something in order to be better. The feeling that one is expected to do something stifles the opportunity for growing at one's own pace and in one's own way. This opportunity or invitation to grow is created by the unconscious realization that is generated by the process of authentic affirmation, "If I am considered lovable in my presently imperfect way, how much more lovable will I be when I outgrow my imperfections!"

It is in this process of affirmation, this process of *knowing and feeling, without doing,* that I give the other to himself. I do not give him his physical existence as a human being. I give him his psychic existence as this specific unique human being. As the popular song expresses it, "You're nobody until somebody loves you"!

The affirming process can be compared in a certain sense, to the effect water has on an object immersed in it. The water surrounds it perfectly and adjusts itself faithfully to the exact contours of the object without destroying it. It allows the object, if a living one, like fish, coral or plant, to grow and develop without hindrance by adjusting its own weight in relation to it. The water cushions with its mass and density any shocks or blows it might receive and thus protects the object. The tiny baby in the water bag of the pregnant mother is an excellent example. Finally, the water may hide from view any defects the object may possess.

COMMUNICATION—COMMUNION

The philosopher-reader may want to go deeper into the meaning of affirmation, by comparing the processes of "communication" and "communion." Nowadays much emphasis is put on communication as the most effective means of greater understanding of one another and thus of better relationships and friendships. In communication we share with one another what we *have:* material possessions, ideas

and thoughts, psychological experiences (e.g. feelings
we have) and spiritual experiences (e.g. our particular religious beliefs).

But what we *are* cannot be communicated. This
is so because there is a profound difference between
having and being. What I *am* can only be received
by the other who gives me his full attention, who
is present to me and becomes aware of what I am,
and that I am good and worthwhile. The other who
wills his awareness of me opens his consciousness
to my being, and comes to know, that is, possess
my goodness. His evident finding delight in my
goodness will be perceived by me. I am revealed to
myself as good. I have received from the other what
I am. I am no longer alone. I have been linked to
another human being in this process of affirmation;
not by communication of what I have, but by the
revelation, the communion of what I am.[6] In friendship the greatest gift my friend can give me is himself. In affirmation I receive an even greater gift:
myself.

In the pages that follow it will become clear that
it is only after I have received myself first that I
can receive the other—man and God—as, so to speak,
additional gifts which complete my happiness.

---

6. See also *New Dynamics in Sexual Love,* by Mary and
   Robert Joyce (Collegeville: St. John's University Press,
   1970). p. 29.

Chapter III

THE OPPOSITE OF AFFIRMATION

The number of unaffirmed people to whom this book is dedicated can be estimated without exaggeration to be in the millions. Moreover, I am certain that this number is growing by the day. This suggests that affirmation is not our usual way of relating to people. How then do most of us ordinarily relate to one another if not in an affirming manner?

Jim, a successful lawyer, but suffering from deep feelings of inferiority and inadequacy, had never been loved by his mother. In fact, she had hated him from the day he was born after failing to abort him with a coat hanger in the third month of pregnancy. His memories of her insane rages and beatings, alternating with cold contempt and neglect of him, were ever vivid in his mind.

Mary, a severely depressed mother of three children, had been raised by a number of baby-sitters, while her parents were seldom home. She had never lacked in material goods, only in love from her socially prominent mother and her too busy father, a nationally known surgeon.

Pat, an unsuccessful suicide, had always received much attention from his mother. She had taken care of his every need, spent hours making him eat everything on his plate, never let him go out on cold days unless bundled up from head to toe, never allowed him to play with the other boys in the street for fear he would be hurt, and rewarded him for never getting his hands or clothes dirty when playing by himself in the yard.

Larry came to my office in his early twenties because he did not know what he wanted to be in life. He was afraid he would not succeed no matter what he did. He had been raised by a kind affectionate mother. His father, however, had always belittled him, had never been satisfied with his grades and reminded him always of the days "when he was a kid and did things so much better." Always ready to criticise and find fault, he rarely ever had complimented Larry for anything, not even for once being the first in his class.

DENIAL

The relationships between Jim, Mary, Pat and Larry and the significant persons in their early lives can be defined best by the word *denial*. Jim had been denied by hate and beatings, Mary by "benign" parental neglect, Pat by smothering love, and Larry by paternal rejection. These are only four of the many ways people deny each other.

Denial as a way of relating to another person seems to be much easier for most of us than affirmation. It almost seems second nature for many of us to spot the faults and shortcomings of another person, and to point them out to him. Whether we do this in order to make him feel ashamed "for his own good" or because we want to appear helpful, it cannot be considered affirmation. And if we claim that we accept another it may be only too often in the expectation that he change and become more like us. But this, too, is denial.

It seems that we want to make ourselves feel better and more important by comparing the other unfavorably with ourselves, by stating directly, or implicitly that we and our ways are the only good ones, that the other's way of being different is a sign of inferiority.

We try to build our own ego by besting the other, by boasting of our greater accomplishments, of our greater strengths and virtues. We do not consider the possibility that our ways may not be superior; our thinking, not the only correct one; our religious beliefs, not the only true ones.

Like the affirming person, the one who denies is also aware of the other's difference, but instead of being delighted by it, it seems to threaten him. It is as if he is not certain of his own goodness and tries to attain certitude by denying the goodness of the other, and demanding that he become like him,

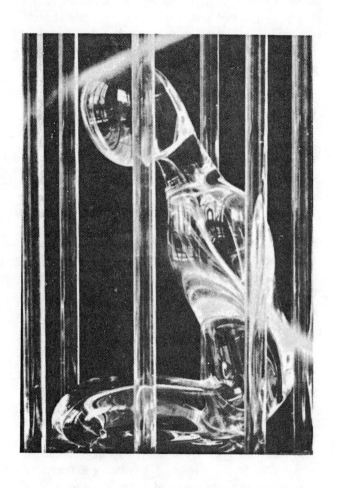

i.e. emulate his own presumed goodness and worth-whileness.

Denial is the hallmark of the immature, the in-secure, the self-centered, the non-affirmed. When Faust, the man who was willing to sell his soul to the devil and condemn himself to hell, asked his visitor who he was, Mephistopheles replied, *"I am the spirit who always denies"!*

What an excellent example of the many profound psychological insights which are to be found in the works of philosophers, dramatists and poets! Goethe realised clearly how denial, more than any other factor, leads to the destruction of what makes each man unique—his human soul or psyche. Thus denial is the cause of a person's psychic death. In denial we push the other away from us; we enlarge the distance between him and ourselves. We be-*little* him by subtracting his faults and shortcomings from what is good in him; we *alien*-ate him from us and push him back into the prison of his loneliness by rejecting him for being different; we cause or contri-bute to his *infirm*-ity by repeatedly focusing on his weaknesses and inadequacies; we *mort*-ify him by humiliating him for his failures.

Denial is the very opposite of affirmation. For it is in being affirmed that man's soul is allowed to flower fully in its own unique way, to become open to its own goodness and that of others. Thus affirmation can be said to be truly lifegiving, and as such the source of another's *psychic incarnation*.

What distinguishes any community, religious or secular, small or large, which possesses this life-giving quality of affirmation is always *pluriformity*. In such communities every person is allowed to be himself because of the sincere, mutual respect and affirmation which transcend color, age, religious beliefs, race or political preference.

POLARIZATION

However, communities where denial prevails are distinguished by the syndrome of polarization. On a large scale polarization sets apart men from women, whites from non-whites, democrats from republicans, conservatives from liberals, over-thirty from under-thirty, one ethnic group from another ethnic group, one religious denomination from another one.

Polarized people are aware of what makes the members of another group different from them, but instead of being moved with respect and admiration, and of finding delight in these differences in the manner that affirming persons do, they primarily, if not solely, respect and admire themselves, and avoid associating with the others. (I refer here, of course, to differences which are more fundamental than personal tastes, preferences, and so on.)

Polarization results from four different forms of denial:
1) Denial through *self-affirmation*[1]

---

1. See Chapter V

2) *Direct* or *indirect* denial by
   a) ignoring another.
   b) drawing attention to another's faults.
   c) belittling the other, back biting, malicious gossip.
   d) unwarranted and tactless criticisms.
   e) ingratitude (even when camouflaged by such socially-stilted phrases as, "You shouldn't have done that!" or "Don't mention it.")
   f) being too busy when the other needs you.
   g) not allowing the other to cry or to show anger or other emotions.
   h) our mistrust, inquisitiveness, checking and spying on the other's actions.
   i) inadequate caring for the other, e.g. when a mother lets her baby drink milk from a bottle propped up on a pillow, while she reads a book.
   j) neglect (Some time ago I saw this poignantly illustrated in a child-care magazine. It was a cartoon of a boy standing by himself at a table on which there was a birthday cake with electric candles and a tape recorder playing, "Happy Birthday.")
   k) frustrating the child's innate need for rational guidance, as for example, when a parent lectures his teenage daughter who is preparing to leave on a date, "And don't sit in the car with your boyfriend in front of the house. I don't want the neighbors to start talking!"
   l) And is it not denial when parents beat their little child for crying or wetting his pants? This form of denial is a numerically significant cause

of non-affirmation, according to a recent newspaper headline stating, "Battered Child Syndrome Reaches Epidemic Proportions. 300,000 children will suffer permanent damage as result of mistreatment this year and another 50,000 will die."

3) Denial by trying to be *neutral* in relating to other people.

For instance, by not wanting to get involved, or by an attitude of "open-mindedness," that never calls for commitment, or by being "tolerant" of what is evil. It should be noted that it is impossible to be neutral in one's association with others. In every relationship with another human being one either affirms or denies. There is no in-between!

4) Denial by *pseudo-affirmation*
This is so easily done:
a) in the casual pat on the shoulder, or the superficial compliment.
b) in the hasty encouragement that is not attuned to the other person's feelings, as for instance when the mother tells her daughter on entering the dentist's office, "Now, there is absolutely nothing to be afraid of, dear."
c) in the premature or too quickly proffered advice that was not preceded by attentive listening. A truly affirming parent is one who, when reasonably possible, drops everything in order to let his child unburden himself or ask questions while giving him his concentrated attention before advising him.

d) in never wanting to hurt the other person's feelings. This may sound strange, yet, if I do this to the point of never letting you know how I feel, and thereby deny you the opportunity of treating me better in the future, I am not affirming you.

e) in permissiveness toward youth. Much of this is merely pseudo-affirmation, since it constitutes the denial of the need of young people for rational guidance by their elders. But adults who unreasonably restrict and confine young people also are offering only pseudo-affirmation.

f) in certain sensitivity training groups, week-end "renewal" sessions, and the like, where the goal is the too rapid liberation of the participants' repressed or retarded emotional lives by various short-term techniques.

g) in paternalism, colonialism, authoritarianism, where one imposes one's own standards of behavior without respect for those being governed.

h) in lowering moral standards and precepts with a mistaken notion that this will help people to become happier and more fulfilled, and prevent neurotic repressions and frustrations. This attitude is prompted by the mistaken belief that the unrestrained experiencing and expressing of all emotions is an absolute prerequisite for growth toward full maturity. This particular form of pseudo-affirmation by promoting objectively unhealthy behavior can be compared to encouraging a little child, who stumbles

and falls in his attempts to walk, to keep on
falling. But if a child were to be encouraged
to keep on falling, he would be denied the
joy of walking erect. Similarly, the person who,
for example, is encouraged to *make love* whenever he wants it, as soon as he wants it, and
with whomever he wants it, will be denied the
joy of *being love.* [2]

i) in "therapeutic" gestures of love which are not
prompted by a sincerely felt and totally unselfish love of the other. When I set out to
affirm you, my patient, in order to experience
your affirmation of me, I fail one of the most
important criteria for being an affirming person, [3] namely, that I be oriented toward you in
a totally unselfish manner. I will receive your
affirmation only when I authentically affirm
you and then only to the extent that you are
ready, able and willing to reveal your knowledge
and feeling of me as being good and lovable
for you. For it is possible for you to withhold
your affirmation of me. However, if you are
willing to let your feelings flow back to me, it
will be the beginning of a mutually affirming
process in which both you and I will grow
toward ever greater happiness.

Although these observations are important

2. See tribute to Gandhi in Chapter VII, The Miracle of
Our Age.

3. See Chapter IV, Portrait of an Affirmed Person

in all relationships, they are especially so in therapeutic ones where the display of degrees and titles by the therapist, and his use of impressive words and terms could conceivably lead an unwary client to expect more than he will receive. The cure of a neurotic individual particularly the deprivation neurotic, is never brought about by techniques or methods, but primarily by the authentic affirmation of the mature, affirmed therapist, not the *pseudo-affirmation* of the *adult-acting* therapist!

Chapter IV

PORTRAIT OF
AN AFFIRMED PERSON

The inmates of the Regina Coeli prison in Rome were gathered in the courtyard under a blue, cloudless sky. It was a very special occasion for them. In front of them stood a man, "a fat man, not handsome, but beautiful, for he was a genius of the heart—maskless".[1]

In the course of his speech he expressed pleasure at this opportunity to visit these incarcerated thieves, murderers, and seducers, and did not hesitate to recall that one of his cousins had once been arrested for poaching and had served a stretch in jail. He concluded by saying, "I have come. You have seen me. I have looked into your eyes. I have placed my heart alongside your heart. Be assured that this meeting will remain deeply engraved in my heart."

---

1. *The Zen of Seeing* by Frederick Franck (Vintage Books, 1973).

Among the prisoners who were allowed to approach
him and kiss his ring were two murderers. One of
them looked up at him with deep sadness on his
face, and asked, "Are those words of hope you
have given us for such a great sinner as I am"?
In response, Angelo Roncalli, better known as Pope
John XXIII bent over the convict and embraced
him.

Whether it was in direct personal contact or via
the television, young and old, men and women,
Catholics and non-Catholics alike all over the world
have been touched and opened by John's affirmation of everyone around him. Many of my patients,
particularly the unaffirmed ones, told me during the
years that John was Pontiff that they were always
deeply moved when they watched him on television.
Some of them would ask me what the reason could
be that this man moved them to tears and made
them feel good and happy with themselves. But most
did not; they "knew" without being able to put it
into words that they were important to John, that
he loved them as they were, that they experienced
the effect of affirmation. People who had met John
in person used to remark that in his presence they
did not feel themselves being judged, but loved for
what they were. John XXIII was the only pope of
modern times about whom an Italian communist
worker could say, "There is a man I'd gladly sit
down to have a drink with"! This pope, this "fat,
but beautiful man", possessed all the qualities of a
man who had been fortunate to be reared by af-

firming parents; and in turn had become an affirmer of man, the things of the world and God.

He was sensitive, open, unselfish, humble and self-restrained, calm and unhurried at all times. He radiated happiness. These qualities, although the direct result of his having been affirmed, could have been either enhanced or obstructed in their development. It is important for the sake of the persons who are still waiting for the gift of their second birth from an affirming other, that we are aware of the various enhancing and obstructing factors operating in our largely neurotic, unaffirmed and unaffirming society.

SENSITIVITY

Early exposure to the many and varied sense objects of this world is necessary for the stimulation and growth of man's external senses. Building castles in the mud, playing in a sandbox, throwing snowballs, swimming, crawling, climbing, running, playing with pets and so on: these things all stimulate and promote the development of the child's senses. This exposure is also provided, and eminently so, in the Montesorri schools for children of kindergarten age.

Play with simple toys and exposure to story telling stimulates the imagination, an important faculty for the development of man's creative talents. Children exposed solely to exact replicas of a fire engine, "sophisticated" dolls, miniature electrical appliances, etc. and spending too many hours watching T.V. will be definitely handicapped in this respect. Nothing is left to the child's imagination. However, by presenting various sense objects to the growing child at the right time in properly graduated quantities, his growing delight in these objects stimulates his desire for further contact with his gradually expanding environment.

The child who is being spoiled, on the other hand, does not get a change to like, desire and appreciate things. This is so because he gets too many toys too early, too abundantly, often before he ever has a desire for them. This child becomes the adult who "buys now and pays later"; who must have everything immediately because he cannot wait. Since the principle of spoiling is not limited to material objects, but extends also to the spiritual realm, excessive and premature exposure to things religious and spiritual will interfere with the development of his sense of wonder and faith.

By exposing the older child to the beauty of the classics, the symphonies, works of art, and so on, his senses will become further refined and his emotional capacity for responding to a greater variety of stimuli larger. Thus his increasing sensitivity makes him more and more capable of being present to the goodness of things and persons, of being aroused by desire for them, and of finding delight and joy in them. This sensitivity will be reflected in the features, bearing and attitude of its owner, just as it was in John XXIII:

"Only very, very rarely have I seen a face that, fully alive, yet without mask—showed the human in all its greatness, without a trace of falsity or pretense. It was in the face of Angelo Roncalli, better known as Pope John XXIII that I saw this pure beauty of the spirit."[2]

"When Pope John examined one of the busts that Manzu had made of him he looked at his image as if absorbing it with all his senses. There was the unguarded open approach of a child whose mind has not been conditioned by school and society to snap open at the known and to narrow down before the unknown. And like a child or any primitive he was instinctively tactile. Noticing how large the sculptor had made his ears, he lifted a hand, his right one with the ruby red ring, to check the enormity of an ear and the thick pendant lobes. At this he smiled again and his eyes had a twinkle of one suddenly meeting some old friend at the bend of the road. He turned then to Manzu with a nod which seemed to indicate they had not seen each other for a long time and had a great deal to talk about. 'How extraordinary is the artist's hand which can create a living work,' said the Pope."[3]

OPENNESS

Being open, not closed off, to all that is good and

---

2. Op. cit. by Frederick Franck

3. *An Artist and the Pope: The Friendship of Manzu and John XXIII* by Peter Davies (London: 1968).

beautiful is a direct consequence of having been affirmed. It is therefore a gift, indeed the *life-giving* gift which must be cherished and protected by refraining from anything, especially the unreasonable demands of society, profession or occupation—that might again undo or reduce this openness. The demands of the office of a pope are great. They could be expected to seriously affect the out-going personality traits of any man. But so great was John's love of all life around him that his openness remained the same throughout his reign. One day when Pope John was at the point of receiving President and Mrs. John F. Kennedy he inquired as to the proper words of addressing the wife of the President of the United States. He was told, "Your holiness can choose either 'Madame President' or simply 'Madame'." But when John entered the audience chamber he spontaneously opened his arms, smiled broadly, and exclaimed, "Ah, Jacqueline."

In October, 1960 two hundred delegates of the United Jewish Appeal, the great American Jewish Welfare Organization, were received in audience by John XXIII in Rome. He welcomed them with opened arms, as he quoted a biblical passage, "I am Joseph, Your brother!"

And when Dr. Arthur Lichtenberger, presiding Bishop of the Episcopal Church of the United States was preparing to kneel when introduced into the presence of the Sovereign Pontiff, the Pope from the far end of his library came toward him with open arms so spontaneously that Dr. Lichtenberger also opened his.

In the open, out-going mode of existence—possessed only by the persons who have been affirmed—we are attentively present to one another, fascinated by what senses, body and spirit reveal in being our authentic selves. In this open existential mode we do not approach one another with preformed ideas and expectations of what we think ought to be. We respectfully listen to what eyes, ears and hands reveal and let these revelations shape our thoughts. We let them reverberate in our emotions which, unless we have been misled to think that these should be repressed, will communicate themselves spontaneously as they always did in John: ". . . Manzu mumbled his thanks and as he began to kiss the papal ring in a gesture of respect and friendship, John drew him close, clasping his shoulder. It was the gesture of a father to his son, an embrace where more questions were asked and more answered than could ever be formed by words."[4]

This openness, which is vastly more encompassing than the popular notion of "open-mindedness," may be blocked or inverted by:

1) self-centeredness

Whenever we are physically sick or disabled our attention will be focused necessarily and primarily on ourselves. Our first concern has to be with our recovery before we can feel free and capable of

---

4. Op. cit. by Peter Davies, page 155

looking outward. Similarly the unaffirmed person cannot help being self-centered as he waits for the door of his lonely prison to be opened from the outside.

2) living in constant fear that something bad may befall us or our loved ones.

Man's astonishing progress in technical know-how has far outdistanced his spiritual growth. Man has become more important than God. In our man-centered society we are forced to rely on man as our savior of all ills. Yet deep inside we are only too aware of our own finite powers and that of other human beings, even when that other is an expert in his field. This, of course, can only create worry and anxiety. A truly *felt* faith and trust in a loving God is essential if we are to become open to the goodness of all being, and to live without fear. However, the presence of this *felt* faith and trust is virtually dependent on and develops only as a result of emotional affirmation. A non-affirmed individual is quite capable of directing his will toward God when his intellect discovers the necessary reasons for doing this. However, purely intellectual orientation toward God does not stimulate his feeling of love for God and does little to open him to knowing and feeling the goodness of all being. In fact, in times of severe emotional stress this spiritual orientation may collapse easily and reveal the underlying fearful self-centeredness.

3) incessant and continued restless striving to attain one's goals and realize one's ambitions.

Excessively ambitious people, and unaffirmed persons striving for self-affirmation, are all victims of our anthropocentric society. Their self-centeredness is not motivated by fear but by energetic striving. Their "tunnel vision" is as much an obstacle to openness as the troubled gaze of the person living in constant worry.

A CALM UNHURRIED WAY OF LIFE

The open, out-going mode of existence changes every human act. It makes us gentle and kind toward ourselves, it allows us time to eat and relax, it allows us quiet during the day as well as at night, a quiet and calm which permits our energy to flow back to its origin and thus to charge us anew.

The busy, driven man cannot be bothered with other people unless they can serve his own utilitarian goals which keep him on the go at all times. The man running through a museum cannot be moved by the beauty of the paintings and sculptures. To the gourmand who gulps his drinks and bolts his food, all foods taste the same. It is quantity he is after, not quality. Only the contemplative person, the connoisseur of art, the gourmet, are aware of the goodness of things, and being moved by this goodness, find joy and happiness.

Quiet as well as silence are essential, too, for only the silent hear. . .what the other has to say. Only the quiet can perceive what the other reveals.

Frederick Franck tells of a woman's comments

after her first lesson in *Seeing/Drawing,* "I am a widow and live alone, and I often feel lonely. Today I learned that if you really see the things around you, you're not lonely anymore!" Affirmation is not limited to human beings. Even in affirming non-living things the affirmer is affirmed in turn, and is not lonely anymore!

UNSELFISHNESS AND HUMILITY

It is not difficult for the unhurried, open, sensitive, well-integrated person to sense where the other is *at,* to see his goodness even if hidden under a mask. But even he must be so unselfish that he finds delight in the goodness of the other without wanting to possess him, without expecting or demanding anything for himself. The truly unselfish person is filled with humble respect and awe for the uniqueness of the other and in his unselfishness leaves it precisely as it is—whole, lovable, admirable. Pope John XXIII was such a man.

"The pope continued to hold on to him. 'As for those who do come into the piazza, my dear Manzu, my poor person really counts for little. We pray together and we look at one another and we say hello. If they find strength in me, I also find it in them. I will tell you even more. I'm a simple brother to them, a brother who became a father by the wishes of our Lord Jesus Christ. Well, all of it, father or brother, depends upon God. What we can do that is important is to continue to love one another, to take hold of what unites

us, leaving aside those little things which might cause trouble, which might turn us against one another.' "[5]

The unselfish person is like the man who looks in admiration at the gold dust in the palm of his hand, and is careful not to try to grasp it and thereby lose it.

Unselfishness is not easy to come by. We are all selfish by virtue of our fallen nature. Yet we can all outgrow it to a large extent (unless we are born psychopathic personalities). Here, too, the road to mature unselfishness would be made so much easier if we received more affirmation.

MORAL SELF-RESTRAINT

An affirmer of man does not give anything that the other cannot accept. He does not demand anything that the other cannot give or do. He refrains from any acts that would be against the moral code especially when the other desires to reciprocate and participate in that act, but has not yet attained sufficient integration and maturity for his emotions to be readily guided by his reason and will.

That affirmer of man adjusts the expression of his love for and delight in the other to the well-being of the other. He practices the highest form

---

5. Op. cit. by Peter Davies, page 56.

of love—the *love of restraint*—which, unfortunately is too often mistaken for repression of feelings, while in fact it is the very opposite!

That affirmer of man has the love of a father who builds a house where the other can be himself, and hide his defects from the world, where he can grow and become who he is *in his way, in his hour,* in the protective humbly serving love of the affirming other.

"Other popes had stood in the same window saying, 'My dearest children,' but Pope John seemed to say it in a different way. Romans and pilgrims from around the world came to listen in wonder as he asked them variously to drive safely, dress warmly, play fair, love one another, and even to pray for a Soviet astronaut. And they came to look at him as though they had lost a father or a brother whom they could find in this house, framed in this window every Sunday at noon."[6]

It is in this very same house that the affirmer, too, in self-restraining love of the other, finds the deepest happiness possible. And it is precisely for this reason that John XXIII not only remained an open person under the heavy weight of his office, but became more open, more happy as the world responded to his affirmation of them by affirming him!

---

6. Op. cit. by Peter Davies, page 54

Chapter V

THE FUTILITY
OF SELF-AFFIRMATION

What would you do if you felt worthless and insignificant as the result of nonaffirmation, and you were endowed with one or more of the following qualities: above average or superior intellect, creative talents, leadership ability, physical beauty, determination, an energetic drive and courage? And what if in addition, circumstances, fate, your lucky star or whatever you want to call it, happened to favor you? What would you do?

You would, I am certain, do what many other unaffirmed individuals have done under those circumstances. You would set out, or more accurately perhaps, be driven to convince yourself, your family, your neighbors, if not the whole world, that you are significant, somebody to be reckoned with—even if nobody loved you. And what do you think your chances of succeeding would be? Wouldn't you expect them to be better than average, even excellent, with so many things going for you—talents,

beauty, intellect, drive and fortuitous circumstances—
and only one thing missing—affirmation?

ADOLF HITLER

Adolph Hitler's father grew up an orphan. He
was an authoritarian figure with a temper to match.
His instant commands had to be obeyed without
fail. Adolf never kept a photograph of his father,
only of his indulgent mother, and on the rare occasions when he spoke of his father it was with
suppressed fury.

Adolf was a mother's boy. She permitted him to
do whatever he wanted in his early years when his
father, whose job as a customs official kept him
away from home for long periods of time, was not
around to chastise him. In later years Hitler often
boasted to one of his personal secretaries—whose
clarity of observation and sensitive intuition made
her in the words of Captain Zoller "an absolutely
reliable witness at the Nüremberg trials"—[1] that
when he was five years old he was still allowed to
sit in his mother's lap. Without a doubt Adolf
Hitler was an inadequately affirmed child. Although
of more than average intelligence he did poorly in
his studies. He failed to pass the entrance examinations for an architectural school in spite of obvious artistic talent, judging by his many doodles
and designs depicted in various biographies. He

---

1. *Douze ans auprès d'Hitler* by Albert Zoller (Paris: Rene
Julliard, 1949).

was largely self-taught through spotty reading, especially of books on history and political science. Years of abject poverty, unemployment, and military service plus time in jail steered this emotionally and academically non-affirmed man toward his ultimate destiny. There is much evidence that he attained his goal as the consequence of a compelling drive to convince himself and the world of his significance and importance, and not as the result of a "stroke of fate," or the machinations of a "criminal psychopath," "insane dictator" or a "Jew-hater with epileptic fits."

The psychoanalyst, Walter C. Langer variously diagnosed Hitler in his secret wartime report, *The Mind of Adolf Hilter*[2] as "psychopathic," "neurotic" and "borderline schizophrenic." These frequently confusing and contradictory diagnostic terms and descriptive labels suggest that there is room for a more accurate and explanatory diagnosis of the personality of the man, Adolf Hitler.

The following recorded observations of Hitler as Führer by his aforementioned personal secretary reveal varied behavioral manifestations typical of a deprivation neurotic, even though they are partly eclipsed by his more spectacular and bizarre conduct. These manifestations suggest how he coped with and compensated for his feelings of loneliness, inferiority and worthlessness. These interpre-

2. New York: Basic Books, Inc. 1972.

tations do not necessarily detract from the specula-
tive value of interesting psychoanalytic interpretations which others have made of his psychosexual
history.

Hitler had a strong will which enabled him to
give up smoking and drinking, and abstain from
meat because of personal convictions (behavior not
typical for a psychopath!). He had a passion for
collecting a variety of things of which he could
not divest himself. He loved to play with his dog
and cat, but had given strict orders to his personal
photographer never to take pictures of them at play.
He had a great fondness for sweets and even in the
last desperate days in the underground bunker when
the city of Berlin was in rubble, Adolf ate cookies
and chocolates by the handful.

He showed a poverty of facial expression. His
personal secretary, Zoller wrote, had seen her em-
ployer smile only a few times in the twelve years
that she worked for him. He was a master in
adapting to the circumstances and changes, however sudden or unexpected, in his life and career
in order to remain in control at all times. Whether
he did this through telling lies, inventing stories,
bluffing or hypocrisy, distorting the truth, false
accusations, and so on, they served the purpose of
manipulating people and events to his advantage
and ultimate control. They are typical of many a
self-affirming person's need to reach his goal of
proving his worth at any price.

Hitler's exaggerated reactions to people who gave

him flowers or gifts are also typical of the unaffirmed person. Hitler often rewarded those people with an abundance of favors for the rest of their lives. His uncertainty about the worth of his own person is demonstrated in the accounts of his personal physician. He was obviously ashamed to undress for a physical check-up and it was always a great effort to exchange his boots for the Bavarian-style leather *hosen* which left his knees bare.

Hitler shrugged off the reports of the tremendous losses of life of his soldiers in the various battles which he misdirected, with the remark, "That's what soldiers are for!" And in response to the reports of the ever growing number of non-combatants who were killed in the Allied bombings of

German cities, callously remarked, "I always told them to build more underground shelters."

How desperate his attempts at self-affirmation must have been was never more clearly demonstrated than by his insistence on personally signing the death sentences of each one of his own generals, some of whom had watched him dance like a child only four years earlier when he received word that France wanted to surrender.

Hitler never married because in his opinion marriage was not compatible with his exalted calling in life and because he did not want to lose the favor of the women voters. However, a more accurate explanation would be the fact that unaffirmed persons are incapable of experiencing the joy of giving and receiving love. Nor is it possible for the other party to find happiness in an intimate relationship with an unaffirmed or deprivation neurotic person. The beautiful Geli, the daughter of Hitler's half-sister and nineteen years his junior, proved this point. She shot herself through the heart not very long after Adolf had fallen in love with her. His only attempt at marriage was with his mistress, Eva Braun, shortly before he killed her and himself. Hitler's attempts at self-affirmation not only had proven futile in the ultimate analysis, but also fatal to himself and his country.[3]

---

3. This information about Hitler's personality is contained in "Peace and Aggression," an address given by Anna A. Terruwe, M.D. to the commanders of the military forces of the Netherlands.

MARILYN MONROE

If it has been easier for people to think of Hitler as a madman, rather than as un unaffirmed individual driven to prove his worth, the opposite holds true for Norma Jean Baker. Her mother, uncle and maternal grandparents were all afflicted with severe mental illness. If anyone could have been expected to develop a psychosis it should have been Norma Jean. Yet there is nothing in her biographies to indicate that she was mentally ill, but everything to show that she was not affirmed.

Norma Jean never knew her father. Shortly after her birth she was boarded out with well-intentioned people who put emphasis on "salvation and the strap." Gladys, her mother, was not able to raise Norma Jean herself since she suffered from loneliness, isolation and rejection. When Norma Jean was nine, just three years after her mother had been taken to the state asylum with paranoid schizophrenia, Norma Jean was dragged to an Orphan's Home, screaming, "I'm not an orphan." Much later she wrote,

> *Don't cry my doll*
> *Don't cry*
> *I hold you and rock you to sleep*
>
> *Hush Hush I'm pretending now*
> *I'm not your mother who died.*

The first time she ever felt loved was when she

was 20, although she had been briefly married at
16. But she had left her husband to live with an
aunt thinking that "she might make a better daughter than a wife!"

"In spite of her considerable emotional deprivation", one of her biographers wrote, "she was
never a complainer." She had spunk and determination enough to try to escape from the Orphans'
Home. She set out to get into the movies on her
own, and she denied herself many things in "her
growing fanaticism about her final success." When
out of movie work at 21, life was bleak. "Unable
to relate to others in any real way" her determination and stubborn will made her persist. She became "the engineer as well as the energizer of her
career," in spite of her insecurity, her hypersensi-
tivity and her mistrust of others.

When Norma Jean became Marilyn Monroe it
meant the abandonment of a hand-me-down kind
of existence. "Although the lifelong quest for af-
fection could not be shaken, she soon felt completely at home with Marilyn, the half-child, half-
woman."

She was always grateful. Six years or so after
Ben Lyon had gotten her her first movie contract
and had given her a fifteen dollar advance on her
salary, she sent him a photograph inscribed: "You
found me, named me and believed in me when no
one else did. My love and thanks forever."

Her beauty and desirability and "her terrible
ambition" never could conceal that she was "rather
like a little frightened animal, a fawn or a baby

chicken," nor that she was "utterly unsure of herself, unable even to take refuge in her own insignificance." In her first meeting with the great moviemaker John Huston "she asked if she could sit on the floor."

The number of her permanent friends "could be counted on the fingers of one hand." There was a "wistful sense of dependency in her that aroused most older women, as well as men of almost any age." Like many an unaffirmed woman, she felt most at ease with children and had no difficulty communicating with them. She was acutely conscious of their needs and knew, too, how to be playful with them.

She loved dogs and cats, and "got wildly involved with her cat's pregnancy, reading up on the subject, watching over her, feeding her extra delicacies. She would interrupt a business session or evening on the town to call her maid and check on kitty".

Her inability to have a child herself was a cruel disappointment to her. "Despite all, she yearned to be a mother, even if it meant temporarily putting films aside. She desperately wanted fulfillment."

Marilyn used every talent she had, her beauty, every ounce of determination, to prove that she was lovable. "She enjoyed the idea of men desiring her; it amused, flattered and excited her. She needed ·that proof of being adored; it denied the inner dread of being unwanted. She sensed love as the hidden miracle in the human scheme. Love, the great equalizer—if we were lucky enough to find it."

"P.S. 'Love me for my yellow hair alone," Marilyn once wrote with trembling hand to Norman Rosten. The actual quote by the great Irish poet, Yeats, a favorite of Marilyn, might have been used as an epitaph:

". . .only God, my dear,
Could love you for yourself alone
And not your yellow hair."

But she never found love, not with Di Maggio, not with Miller, not with others, even those who were ready "to listen, to smile or laugh, to argue, to create a human environment." As soon as she was alone "the void opened up before her, endless and terrifying."

What Marilyn needed was authentic affirmation. If she got this from some, especially the motherly and fatherly figures in her life, it must have been more than offset by others who saw her only as a sex symbol, or tried to exploit her, or put her down. Consistent, authentic affirmation by someone able to protect her from the pseudo-affirmation and denial of others would have been her only opportunity to find herself. It is heartening to read that her psychoanalyst went out of his way to affirm and protect her. But it proved to be too late. Rosten quotes Dr. Greenson, the analyst, as saying, "It may seem odd to you the method I am using to treat her, but I firmly believe that the treatment has to suit the patient and not vice-versa. Marilyn is not an analytic patient, she needs psychotherapy, both supportive and analytical. I have permitted her to become friendly with my family and to visit in my home because I felt she needed actual experiences in her life to make up for the emotional deprivation she had suffered from childhood onward. It may seem to you that I have broken rules, but I feel that if I am fortunate enough, perhaps some years from now, Marilyn may become a psychoanalytic patient. She is not ready for it now. I feel I can tell you these things because she considers you and Hedda her closest friends and there must

be somebody with whom I can share some of my
responsibilities."[4]

Marilyn was 36 when she died of an overdose
of sleeping pills. Her hand hung limp on one of
her telephones, the phone which had been an ally
against loneliness for her nearly all of her life.[5]

> *Help   Help*
> *Help   I feel life coming closer*
> *When all I want is to die.*
> — *Marilyn Monroe*

Adolf Hitler and Marilyn Monroe were successful
in attaining what they thought would take away the
pain of feeling worthless, unwanted and unloved.
But neither Adolf's awesome power which made
him respected and feared by millions, nor Marilyn's

---

4. These remarks by Dr. Greenson point out correctly that
   a person may have a combination of two neuroses, namely
   a classical, Freudian repressive neurosis superimposed
   on a deprivation neurosis. The latter often predisposes
   the person to the development of the former. Although
   each type of neurosis requires a totally different therapeutic approach, they can often be dealt with in therapy
   at the same time, as long as the patient's need for affirmation is gratified continuously and consistently at
   all times. I am inclined to believe from what I have read
   that Marilyn Monroe had only a deprivation neurosis.

5. Most of the information on Marilyn Monroe has been
   quoted from *Norma Jean-The Life of Marilyn Monroe*
   by Fred Lawrence Guiles (New York: Bantam Books,
   Inc., 1970) and *Marilyn, An Untold Story* by Norman
   Rosten (New York: New American Library, Inc. 1973.).

captivating beauty and her countless admirers were able to kill the pain of not having received the gift of themselves from an affirming other. Hitler destroyed many before killing himself. Marilyn hurt no one, she killed only herself.

Such is the tragedy of the unaffirmed person's attempts at self-affirmation. He is doomed to failure, no matter whether:

1) he succeeds in amassing material possessions which are the envy of the Jones' next door, or in becoming a millionaire many times over, able to buy anything he desires; or

2) he is successful in his studies and able to display and use an impressive array of degrees and titles which open the doors of academic institutions and invite solicitations to important faculty posts;

   (One psychiatrist I knew had no less than seventeen degrees, certificates of membership in professional organizations and distinguished awards adorning the otherwise bare walls of his office. This impressive number of framed pieces of paper was a most accurate gauge of the depth of his loneliness and feelings of inferiority.)

3) he reaches the top of the ladder in his business, profession or vocation;

   (I saw many wives and children of the world's top specialists—all victims of their husband's and fathers' inability to affirm them. There are many among the hierarchy of the Church who reached their exalted positions because of organizational talents and seniority. Their lack of affirming, fatherly qualities had its share in the crisis in the priesthood and aggravated their own inner loneliness and isolation from their people.)

4) he attains national or international fame, or if that proves impossible he does the next best thing, he associates with famous people;

(Many unaffirmed men and women are to be found in show business. To them the acclaim they receive from their audiences "proves" that they are worthwhile, significant and lovable. Yet one famous and successful comic has been reported to suffer the agonies of the damned for the entire period between his weekly T.V. shows, each one a tremendous success for years and years. Yet he always feared that his audiences would not laugh, would not applaud, would frustrate his need to be told that he was somebody!)

5) he gains power over others in positions of authority, political life, dictatorship, secret police and concentration camps, syndicates or gangsterism;

In my psychiatric practice I have seen many unaffirmed members of religious communities of men or women, both superiors and subjects. Those who had risen to the top used their authority to retain their power demanding and receiving blind obedience of their unaffirmed subjects. The latter were usually persons who had joined their religious communities in the hope of finding a sense of belonging, of being loved and taken care of. However, they often discovered to their chagrin that the non-affirming Superior was more "superior" than "mother" or "father." Both the superiors and the subjects in these communities were unhappy and unaffirmed people.

I also observed an unusually large number of unaffirmed people among teachers and professors. Even though they derived a sense of importance from the obedience and docility of their students this never brought them the feeling of being worthwhile and significant for being who they were. There were also many teachers who sought my help because they were unable to maintain proper discipline in their classes.

6) he engages in homosexual or heterosecual promiscuous behavior.

From my clinical observation such behavior more often than not has its origin in a desperate search for the love never received from an affirming other. The futility of this search is demonstrated by the endless cruising engaged in by many homosexuals, and in the pre- and extra-marital sexual promiscuity of both single and married people. The sexually promiscuous person perpetuates his own frustration because as long as he does not call a halt to his genital activity, he will never be convinced that he is lovable for being himself instead of for his body.

Many unaffirmed individuals use two or more of the aforementioned six means to affirm themselves.

When it is power, position of authority and superior intelligence which are used in combination the effects can be far reaching. They can be even disastrous when that individual is a clever, cunning, and ruthless person who is able to deceive and manipulate others under the guise of being reliable, trustworthy and honest. At times it will be extremely difficult to distinguish such a person from a psychopathic liar or paranoid psychopath. The danger of such a cleverly manipulating self-affirming individual suffering ultimately a psychotic breakdown is, in my opinion, considerable.

I trust that I have not conveyed the impression that all very rich people, teachers, bishops, superiors or show business people are unaffirmed persons! For even though this would not be anything shameful it would be inaccurate. Nor is it correct to assume that self-affirmation is always an unhealthy or futile psychological process. The truly mature, affirmed person's awareness of and respect for his own goodness and worth is a healthy form of self-affirmation, of unselfish self-love.

This strictly circumscribed aspect of self-affirmation as a healthy process is to be distinguished from Rollo May's understanding of self-affirmation.[6] Since there is too much at stake in terms of the psychic

---

6. *Power and Innocence,* A Search for the Sources of Violence (N.Y.: W. W. Norton & Co., 1972).

health of individuals, communities, societies and countries, I must take issue with his claim that "self-affirmation and self-assertion are essential to humanity."[7] Of course, I have no quarrel with "self-assertion being essential to humanity." even though May defines self-assertion as "a stronger more overt form of self-affirmation and. . .a potentiality in all of us that we react to attack."

But it is impossible to subscribe to his definition of self-affirmation as "the second of man's five levels of power." The reason for May's confusing use of these terms is undoubtedly the fact that he does not define the term "affirmation" in his book. When he uses the term "affirmation" it is in the sense of "assert" or "love." Thus he is certainly correct in pointing out that it is "puritanical to deny self-affirmation on moral gounds," but here he explicitly means self-love.

Even though May writes somewhere that "the sense of worth of oneself is coming from other people" (and thus affirmation in my use of the term), the tenor of his book is that "it is basically one's own efforts that determine whether one is worthwhile or not." This is strikingly brought out when he writes, "It is tragic indeed when whole peoples are placed in a situation where significance becomes almost impossible to achieve. The blacks are, of course, the most ready illustration. The central crime. of the white man was that he placed the blacks dur-

---

7. Op. cit., page 23.

ing several centuries of slavery and one century of physical freedom, but psychological oppression, in situations where self-affirmation was impossible. In physical slavery and later in psychological slavery every one of the known violent phases was difficult or impossible. They were permitted to affirm themselves only as singers, dancers, and entertainers for the titillation of the white man or as tillers of the white man's fields, and later in the construction of the white man's automobiles. That this would lead to widespread apathy and later on to radical explosion should no longer surprise anyone."

In other words, May seems to say that if the blacks had been permitted to affirm themselves as doctors and engineers and astronauts, etc., they then would really have attained a sense of significance, a sense of being worth while. This again, of course, proves the fallacy of his theory of self-affirmation. There are many, many people who have achieved great fame, fortune, renown, etc. and still have no feeling of being worthwhile and significant.

It would be hard to imagine that Rollo May has never seen persons who have striven all their lives to affirm themselves—and successfully so—in the sense that they proved to others that they were significant, yet suffer from unabated feelings of inferiority and worthlessness. The only explanation for this seeming paradox—feelings of inferiority and a poor self-image in people who are recognized by the world as superior and important persons—is lack of authentic affirmation.

Or did May sense the difference, after all, between

affirmation and self-affirmation, but fail to bring it out by not defining his terms properly? For he also wrote, "When Priscilla remarked to me that a man in her hometown would not have committed suicide if 'one person had known him ," what was she saying? I believe she was saying that this man had no person to whom he could open himself. No one was interested enough in him to listen, to pay attention to him. She was saying that he lacked someone who had compassion for him, a compassion which would be the basis of his self-esteem. If he had had such a person he would have counted himself too valuable to wipe out."

Priscilla was right!

Chapter VI

FROM DEPRIVATION
TO AFFIRMATION—
WHAT CAN YOU DO FOR
YOURSELF AND OTHERS?

"A Dutchman can look a cat out of the tree"!
This is what natives of the Netherlands say about
themselves. No wonder that I, born and raised in
that little country, still smile each time I lecture on
a subject as for example, the causation, treatment
and prevention of the neuroses and someone in
the audience stands up and asks eagerly, "Doctor,
what can we do"? I usually reply, "Nothing—at
least not right away! Let the ideas I presented here
sink in first, ponder them at your leisure, until
you start to develop some feelings about them. Once
you are emotionally aroused by these ideas it will
be time for you to start doing something"!

Being always precedes doing. And feelings should
precede most of our doing especially when we are

still children. The older we become the more our feelings should be joined by our thinking before we act. The consequences of acting contrary to this existential principle are striking as far as our use of words is concerned. We all know from personal experiences that the saying, "Sticks and stones may break my bones, but words will never hurt me," has little truth. Words can not only hurt, they can mortally wound the other person's psyche. This happens when the words of affirmation are not spoken when they should be, and when the words of denial are not held back in loving self-restraint. The same is true for our use of words that are devoid of feeling. The French language lends itself well to bring out the difference between "the spoken word" and "the word that speaks", "la parole parlée" and "la parole parlant"!

One of the first things you should concentrate on when you are unaffirmed is to:
1) **Be yourself.**
This means to be *honest* with your feelings and opinions. After all, if and when somebody indicates that he loves you, you do not want to have to torture yourself with the thought, "Would he still love me if he knew what my *real* feelings are? Would it make any difference to him if he knew that I am angry at him, or do not agree with his thinking, or dislike something he did?" Yet, these are the things which are kept hidden by the majority of unaffirmed people in their eagerness to be loved and accepted for what they are. But if you

agree that you want to be loved for yourself and not for what you pretend to be, it follows that you must be yourself!

Of course, this will scare you at first, especially if you have trained yourself for years to behave in the way you think others expect a *nice* person to behave. If so, you can make things easier for yourself by answering the question, "What really have I accomplished by always being so *nice*, and never letting on to my real feelings and thoughts"? The chances are that you will have to admit that even if you have no real enemies, and everyone seems to like you for being so *nice* you have no real, close, intimate and reliable friends. This will be so even if you become an expert at willing the expression of the emotions which you don't feel, or repressing those you are afraid to feel. Sooner or later every unaffirmed individual discovers the tragedy of the whole masquerade of being so *nice* that he is still where he started—unloved! Every unaffirmed person comes to realize that he has gained nothing by trying to be someone other than himself. In fact, many become confused and wonder, "If nobody loved me when I was young and myself, why is it that now after trying so hard for years to please everyone and to be *nice,* still nobody loves me?" So, dare to be yourself so thoroughly, so authentically that you will be free to turn out of yourself toward the other, free to discover his goodness without seeing it as a potential threat, free to affirm him—or not.

In order to become your real self, you need courage to:
2) **stop hiding or repressing your emotions.**
This does not mean that you should start to express them immediately either. Before you do this take plenty of time, days, weeks, or months, if necessary, to reassure yourself inwardly, over and over, that it is good to feel whatever emotions you feel. Once you feel comfortable with the emotions you used to fear, you are ready to begin experimenting in expressing them. You will learn that each emo-

tion can be expressed in many more ways than you ever thought possible.

It is especially necessary to stop repressing those emotions which you and so many people with you mistakenly consider "negative" or "bad" emotions, like hate and anger. However, there are no negative or bad emotions! *All emotions are good!*[1] All emotions are necessary, and serve specific functions in your overall living as a mature human being. As long as you do not or cannot use effectively emotions such as hate—merely a stronger word for dislike—and anger, you are crippled in defending yourself against harmful things; you are disabled in being stimulated to overcome handicaps and obstacles that separate you from the things you desire, from the things that will make you happy.

Strange as it may seem to you at first, the emotions of hate and anger are your friends. If you want to really love and to be loved, if you want to be really joyful and have courage, then you must feel comfortable also with the emotion of hate for what is not good or lovable; in feeling the emotion of anger when you are treated shabbily, unjustly, or are slighted or manipulated.

As far as your emotional life is concerned, *it is all or nothing.* You either feel all your emotions

---

1. Human love has two elements: emotional love and volitional love (an act of the will). Likewise human hate has the same two elements: hate as pure feeling or emotion, and hate as an act of the will.

fully or all of them poorly, or even not at all. You cannot pick or choose from the set of emotions which each person is born with and which is fundamentally the same in every man. If fact, since it is against your nature to pick or choose, you will pay the price for doing so with constant tension, restlessness, anxiety, and a host of possible psychosomatic troubles.

To summarize very briefly, what has been described in great detail in *Loving and Curing the Neurotic,* emotions are *motors.* They are there to move you, or for you to be moved by them. The emotions of love, desire and joy are there so you can *be moved* by the goodness of all that is good and pleasurable, to be emotionally involved in what is good for you. This kind of movement is expressed for example in "a moving performance."

Similarly the emotions of hate, aversion and sadness serve the purpose of your feeling, of your being moved by what is not good, not pleasurable for you. "I was moved to tears." These feelings, then, may be followed by your *doing* something if your reason deems it advisable and proper.

The other emotions of hope, courage, fear, despair and anger are there to *move you,* to stimulate the muscles of your extremities, the muscles involved in speech and writing. Then with the consent and cooperation of your reason and will—or for that matter without them—you can act towards overcoming obstacles that stand between you and the object of your desire, or towards protecting yourself against something harmful.

However, whether you act or not, and how, is entirely another matter and is secondary, i.e. subsequent to the emotions, to what you feel. The decision to do something, and how and when, is entirely up to your common sense, your reason, and your evaluation of the present in the light of what you recall about similar situations of the past. Your fear should never be the deciding factor!

Always remember that your emotions are one thing, your actions are another. They should be linked by reason and will, not by fear! Your emotions are outside of the realm of moral judgment.

Since one of the main reasons for repressing and not using your emotions fully is your own fear of your emotions, it is important that you:

3) **Do not hang on to your fears** especially the fear of hurting other people's feelings.

This fearful attitude has become a widespread, almost fashionable concern among people today. It stems from the mistaken belief that it is the highest virtue to go to any length to be considerate of the feelings of other people. Actually it is merely a pseudo-Christian virtue not practiced by Christ in his life on earth. He always said and did what he knew was right even if it would hurt someone's feelings. In my clinical practice of psychiatry, I have found the term *hurting other people's feelings* to be almost always synonymous with *irritating people, making people angry.* And likewise *I was so hurt* means *I was so irritated, annoyed or angry.*

Once you learn to identify your *hurt* as being actually *anger* you should make it a practice to call a spade a spade. For as long as you speak of yourself as being *hurt* you'll have an image of yourself being struck down, helpless, paralyzed, waiting for someone to come to your rescue. Even if you know better, this subconscious association with your use of the word *hurt* will cause you to feel helpless and weak. Your use of the word *anger,* on the other hand, will create a subconscious image of readiness to fight and defend yourself and therefore will cause you to feel courageous.

Unaffirmed individuals whose way of living is determined or dominated by this fear of hurting other people's feelings are afraid of making people angry at them, as anger for them excludes love, the love they so desperately crave. Moreover, they thus hope not to be aroused to anger in turn, since they themselves don't know how to cope with it. I have discussed the subject of how to cope with anger effectively in great detail elsewhere.[2]

So instead of trying to protect yourself through your fear, learn to *live dangerously*—that is, dangerously for you!—by doing and saying what you think, know or believe is right, by not caring that you may be mistaken at times, by relying on the motor of your emotions under the slowly growing guidance of your reason and common sense, in order to

---

2. See *Loving and Curing the Neurotic*

maintain yourself as yourself, as the unique human being you are supposed to be. This is frequently the most difficult thing to do for those people who have learned to *short-circuit* their emotions by means of the following reasoning process. "I feel irritated when he slurps his soup. But he is feeling blue and if I were to show how I feel he would get more depressed. So, I'll ignore my feeling of irritation." Or someone may reason, "I would like to invite Mary out to dinner. But if I do, she may wonder why, and her friend Jean may be unhappy that I did not invite her, too, and so-and-so will wonder what's going on, etc. So I'd better not ask Mary out for dinner." These persons must learn to rea- son less, and dare to follow their first feeling impulse. They must learn to *jump before they look!*

Instead of using your energy in fearfully imagin- ing all the bad things that possibly could happen to you, use it to imagine yourself acting and speaking assertively, to imagine people congratulating you on speaking your mind, to imagine people treating you with respect when you act assertively, to imagine yourself coping effectively with unpleasant situations. This is the *power of positive imagining,* a much more effective way than the power of positive thinking, especially when you practice this frequently in a fully relaxed state.[3]

---

3. In order to help you do this more easily I have made a 3 cassette tape set which will teach you how to develop

If unaffirmed you must learn to:
4) be assertive.

This is another way of expressing what I said about *"living dangerously."* If you understand the proper distinction between aggression and assertion,[4] you will agree that it is natural for you to assert yourself. Therefore employ every avenue to learn to do this as part of being yourself. If you have been afraid that this would cause you to blow your top each time you become angry, remember that your risk of being explosively angry just when you least expect it is greatest when you persist in your attitude of fear or determination never to be angry! You can freely decide not to show your anger, or to show your anger in this way or that way, only when: a) you have learned to feel comfortable with all your emotions—your feeling of love as well as hate, your feeling of courage as well as anger, and b) when they have been given plenty of opportunities over the years to interact readily and smoothly with your faculties of reason and will.

For this you need practice, courage and determination to break:

---

your power of positive imagination through body and mind relaxation and other special techniques. Information on these tapes, entitled "Affirmation and Psychic Incarnation for Emotionally and Spiritually Troubled Persons", may be obtained by sending a stamped, self-addressed envelope to the author, Conrad W. Baars, M.D., 326 Highview Drive, San Antonio, Texas 78228

4. See Addendum I

The non-assertive person's *vicious circle of feeling unloved.*

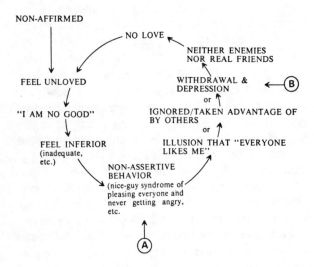

A marks the first spot to break the vicious circle, e.g. by daring to disagree, giving an honest compliment, volunteering self-praise, being honest with your feelings in your words and actions, not repressing your feelings of annoyance or anger, etc., etc.

B marks the second spot where you can break the vicious circle of feeling unloved. Depressed people often wonder why they feel blue. Things seem to be going fairly well, yet they feel depressed. One sure way to get to the root of the trouble is by asking themselves not, "Why do I feel blue?", but, "What or who is irritating me?" More often than not they will realize that they do feel irritated, but have been unwilling or afraid to recognize this fact because they are so uncomfortable with feeling angry or irritated.

Even in therapy patients who are learning to apply this technique successfully will not infrequently backslide when they do not apply it to "those little things that shouldn't bother me." But as soon as they realize that this attitude is wrong and do something to change it, they are on the permanent road to freedom from depression. Every emotion of anger, whether caused by "big" or "little" things must first be *felt, accepted* and *respected*. Only then is reason free to perform its proper function of deciding how to deal most effectively with the cause of the anger. Since the forementioned requires much energy, it is essential that you:

5) **do not bend over backward to please everyone** (unless, of course, you are already a fully mature, freely self-determining person).

It is futile to try to please everyone, to try to have peace at any price from fear that you will not be loved. It never assures you of getting what you desire—to be loved for yourself—and besides it is impossible to please everyone. By always trying to please everyone you waste a tremendous amount of energy, which you can use a lot better, for instance, in learning to feel comfortable with all your emotions and in practicing to be assertive.

Chronic alcoholics or people relying too much on their daily dose of this liquid tranquilizer can benefit from the clinical observation that the unaffirmed person's non-assertive life style creates considerable tension. Since alcohol is the ideal substance to dissolve this tension—though only temporarily, of course —they will derive much benefit from following the guidelines in this chapter. In my psychiatric practice I have found that the majority of chronic alcoholics are unaffirmed people.[5]

One way of preserving your energy is by:

6) **not trying to make yourself seem more important** by putting other people down or needlessly criticizing them.

If you cannot say anything kind to or about a person, at least do not say the usual nasty or belittling things, nor the pseudo-affirming and pseudo-helpful things like "Don't cry, dear"; "Oh, it is nothing" (when someone pays you a compliment); "You shouldn't feel like that, sweetheart"; "Don't mention it" (when someone thanks you); "You ought to do something about your temper"; "Say 'thank you' to Aunt Mary for the nice present, Johnny." The least you can do for yourself and for society in this matter of affirmation—even as an unaffirmed person—is to stop denying others. If the life-giving process of mutual affirmation is to

---

5. See: "The Alcoholic Priest", by Conrad W. Baars, M.D. in *The Priest*, Vol. 27, No. 6, 1971

start, then the self-feeding process of mutual denial
has to be broken somewhere.

Instead of relating to others in a non-affirming
or denying way,

7) **be constantly on the lookout for what is good**
in other people.

No matter how well hidden it may be, it can be
found! Then reveal it—affirmingly! Try to become
an expert at it! You can and should apply this to
yourself also, provided you:

8) **stop thinking that you are no good,** and are
worth nothing because your parents or other
significant people in your earlier life did not succeed in making you feel loved.

If those persons did not affirm you it might have
been because they themselves were never loved or
because they were emotionally repressed, rigid, and
fearful of their emotions; or they were too busy
to love you adequately; or they resented your birth
for selfish motives; or they were simply blind to
your lovableness. But whatever the reason, it was
never because you were not lovable, good or worthwhile! One thing is certain, your parents were deprived, or deprived themselves, of the joy of loving
you, of being affirmed by your smile when you felt
loved by them! They were the losers by not being
sensitive and open to your unique worth and goodness. They lost just as much, if not more than you
did in not being affirmed by them.

It is all right for you to feel sorry for them, or

to feel hate for them, or to feel angry or resentful at them. As I said before, all these feelings are emotions and thus outside the realm of morality and guilt! But stop thinking that their actions were caused by your being no good or worthless. Actually it happened the other way around. It was *their* actions and attitudes which made you feel worthless, and then these feelings, in turn, led you to think that you were. Most children are inclined to think," after all, how can adults be wrong?"— Well, by now you and I know how stupid, sick and wrong selfish adults can be.

9) **don't expect to find authentic affirmation in bed** with just anyone.

When sex comes into the picture, you will be asking yourself sooner or later, "Would he love me if he could not have sexual relations with me?" Sex by its very nature is primarily sought for selfish reasons even when shared with someone else, though then it is, of course, more enjoyable—just like a gourmet dinner. But it can and does become an additional expression of unselfish love, and thus of greater happiness, once the bonds of love and friendship have been formed and tested without genital involvement. This, of course, requires an advanced degree of maturity. But it is precisely this level of maturity which makes it possible and not too difficult to refrain from genital activity when not to abstain would introduce not only an element of selfishness or disregard of established moral codes, but also would constitute a defect in the mutual affirmation which is the source of all happiness. I am referring, of course, to the need to refrain from genital involvement *periodically* during marriage for the purpose of spacing pregnancies or for other reasons, or *permanently* in the celibate state of life, in friendships between men and women outside marriage, or in friendships between persons of the same sex. The joy experienced in this *self-restraining love* is the most profound man can know.

10) **Stop trying to affirm yourself,** to prove to yourself and the whole world that you are worthwhile and good. Although I have discussed this extensively in the previous chapter, I just wanted to remind you again! Only another human being can affirm you; only another person can give you to yourself. For him you can only:

11) **wait in patience, unhurriedly,** in openness, while living your own life in your own unique way, daring to be yourself, stifling your fear of the adult world, in the realization that for a large part it is only a seemingly adult world you live in.

If the people around you were really adults, that is, mature, fully grown, and unselfish, they would affirm you, allow you to be yourself, and love you because you are different and unique. Remind yourself often of this sad truth: that most people around you are in the same boat as you are and that their boat may be even more leaky and less seaworthy than yours. Those who are trying to keep from drowning by attempts at self-affirmation will frighten you in their behavior unless you realize what is going on. You can either act like them and thus keep the process of denying one another going, or you can break the vicious circle with the knowledge and courage you have gained in this book. Your simply not denying others will, when others join you in ever growing numbers, open the way to mutual affirmation and thus to human happiness.

Therefore your contribution as an unaffirmed person to the well-being and happiness of society should not be underestimated! Without your openness the affirming person's love is frustrated. In this sense he is dependent on you, just as much as you are dependent on him for affirmation! In the matter of affirmation we are all each other's masters and subjects at the same time!!

Since affirmation is for everyone, in all relationships, in all life situations, none of us can afford not to do his part, whether at home, in the neighborhood, at school, in business, in a profession, in politics, in government, in international relationships or in the churches. We particularly need affirmed and affirming leaders in all these areas! Affirmation cannot be confined to the psychiatrist's office. For each and everyone of us there is a task greater than that of the psychiatrist, counselor or welfare worker. It is the task of being a creator, a giver of the other's psychic existence in joy and happiness!

12) **Therefore, be gentle with yourself** and with the child-like feelings within you—they have a right to be there and to grow and catch up with the rest of you that is already grown!

Chapter VII

AFFIRMATION
—THE MIRACLE OF OUR AGE

Much has been written about the life of John XXIII. In chapter four we have shown him in life as an affirmed person. The following reflections by Manzu on his departure from this life show the recognition of John's affirming greatness among people throughout the world.

"It seemed to him at that moment that once or twice in a generation a dying monarch or a dead hero is picked to represent the dignity and continuity of a nation's life. This was happening now, not just in this ancient cobblestoned oval, but far beyond it, in other piazzas, in homes, in chapels around the world, while millions of people had followed this death, step by step. Their mumbled prayers down muted stairs were more than strangled goodbyes. They were a massive vote, an act of belief that divisional hatred was not the only reality of the human condition. There was something else in all men, however prone to evil. It was this which went out from him, touching all classes of people, all colors and castes and creeds. It echoed in the hearts of all as in one heart, proved that all variety of man belonged to one human family. It came as a relief at a terrible time of the world when some were saying that man was incapable of reason and unable to control his destiny. It said there was a chance and that we would not despair. It gave man a kind of glimpse of how the world would look if it were governed by love. And it was this glimpse which had brought all ages and faiths of men into the piazza to look up at the window of the man whose life and death bearing witness of this truth, was a miracle of our age."

This life and death—this affirmation—a miracle of our age! Indeed! But John was not the only man to embody this miracle. There have been others.

CHRIST AFFIRMS

One of them, Christ, is the perfect representation of an affirmed and affirming person. I quote a few

---

1. Op. cit. pg. 246

New Testament examples of the finely attuned and exquisitely gentle ways in which this extraordinary figure, the eternal source of all affirmation, affirmed all people. He loved each person precisely as he was.

Christ affirmed Simon Peter knowing he would be denied by him three times before the cock crowed: Instead of turning his back on him He told him, "You are Peter and on this rock I will build my church." He affirmed him tenderly in his weakness.

He affirmed Mary Magdalen, the woman who had a bad name in the town. At the dinner in the house of Simon the Pharisee, Christ turned toward the woman and said to Simon, "Do you see this woman? I entered your house, you gave me no water for my feet, but she has wet my feet with her tears and wiped them with her hair. You gave me no kiss, but from the time I came in she has not ceased to kiss my feet. You did not anoint my head with oil, but she has anointed my feet with ointment. Therefore I tell you her sins which are many are forgiven for she loves much; but he who is forgiven little loves little." And he said to the woman, "Your faith has saved you. Go in peace."

Zaccheaus, the chief tax collector, was another who was affirmed by Christ. When Christ saw him in the sycamore tree where Zaccheaus, being small of stature, had climbed in order to see him better, Christ said to him, "Zacchaeus, make haste and come down, for I must stay at your house today";

and Zaccheaus responded to the Lord's affirmation
of him with the words, "Behold, Lord, one half
of my goods I will give to the poor; and if I have
defrauded anyone of anything I will restore it four-
fold."

He affirmed the children who were turned away
by the disciples by saying, "Let the children come
to me; do not stop them; for it is to such as these
that the kingdom of God belongs."

Meeting the tax collectors and sinners, Christ
said, "It is not the healthy who need the doctor,
but the sick. Go and learn the meaning of the
words: 'What I want is mercy, not sacrifice!' And,
indeed I did not come to call the virtuous but the
sinners."

At the moment that Judas betrayed Jesus with a
kiss, he said, "My friend, do what you are here
for." Not even then did he speak words of condem-
nation.
—He appeared to Thomas who could not believe
that Christ was risen, and affirmed him in his doubt,
"Put your fingers here: look here are my hands.
Give me your hand and put it into my side. Doubt
no longer, but believe."

When Martha complained to Jesus that her sister
had left her to do the serving all by herself, he said,
"Martha, Martha, you worry and fret about many
things, yet few are needed; but only one thing is
necessary."

The woman at the well, a Samaritan with whom Jews did not associate was affirmed by Christ with the words, "Give me a drink of water," and after she had admitted to having no husband, "You are right to say, 'I have no husband,' for although you have had five, the one you have now is not your husband. You spoke the truth there."

Christ affirmed the woman caught in adultery by pointing out her relative goodness, "Let him who is without sin among you be the first to cast a stone at her.", and with his gentle words, "Woman, where are they? Has no one condemned you?". . ."Neither will I condemn you." It was only after these words of affirmation that he added, "Go your way, and sin no more."

In the Parable of the Prodigal Son, who sinned against heaven and his father, it was the father who loved his son just the way he was. "His father saw him while he was still a long way off; he ran to the boy, clasped him in his arms and kissed him tenderly."

To the thief on the cross who asked Christ to remember him Christ said, "Indeed, I promise you, today you will be with me in paradise."

Elsewhere we read of Saul who had been persecuting Christians. On his journey to Damascus Paul was blinded by a light from heaven, fell to the ground and heard a voice saying to him, "Saul,

Saul, why do you persecute me?" And he said, "Who are you, Lord?" And the Lord said, "I am Jesus whom you are persecuting. It's hard for you to kick against the goad." And immediately Paul surrendered his will and asked, "What must I do?"

Christ himself asked for affirmation when, after they had finished breakfast on the lake shore, he asked Simon Peter three times, "Simon, son of John, do you love me more than these?" And Peter replied three times, "Yes, Lord, you know everything, you know that I love you".

And on another occasion when Jesus put this question to his disciples, "Who do you say that I am?" Simon Peter spoke up, "You are the Christ, the Son of the Living God!" and Jesus replied, "Simon, son of John, you are a happy man!"

GOD THE FATHER AFFIRMS

The very first example of affirmation recorded in the Scriptures was when God, in the process of creating the earth, paused each evening of every day, "And God saw everything that he had made, and behold, it was very good."

We know of four occasions when God himself affirmed his Son. First at his Baptism when a voice was heard from heaven saying, "This is my beloved Son, with whom I am well pleased." This was the Father's declaration of love for his Son.

The second affirmation was on Mount Tabor, when he affirmed Christ in his deeds as a teacher, "This is my beloved Son with whom I am well pleased; hear him."

Later on towards the end of his life, in Gethsemani no human being could give Jesus in his agony the affirmation he needed. That is why the apostles were asleep. He received consolation from the angel, sent to the garden by the Father. The essence of this consolation is that his suffering was affirmed as good. And when Christ had received that consolation he was able to undergo the suffering. He responded, "Your will be done."

And the ultimate affirmation was the Resurrection through which Christ was given life, and mankind was opened to real life—our Redemption.

GANDHI AND KASTURBAI

I conclude this chapter with a brief, but beautiful reference to what must have been two affirmed and affirming historical figures, Mohandes Karamchand Gandhi, better known as Mahatma (great-souled) Gandhi, Hindu nationalist and spiritual leader, and his wife of sixty years of happy married life—Kasturbai.

These are the words Kasturbai addressed to her husband whom she had followed to prison, with whom she had shared his three week fasts, and with whom she had taken a vow of celibacy after the birth of their four sons.

"I thank you for having had the privilege of being your lifelong companion and helpmate. I thank you for the most perfect marriage in the world, based on *brahmacharva* (self-control) and not on sex. I thank you for having considered me your equal in your life work for India. I thank you for not being one of those husbands who spend their time in gambling, racing, women, wine, and song, tiring of their wives and children as the little boy quickly tires of his childhood toys. How thankful I am that you were not one of those husbands who devote their time to growing rich on the exploitation of the labor of others.

"How thankful I am that you put God and country before bribes, that you had the courage of your convictions and a complete and implicit faith in God. How thankful I am for a husband who put God and his country before me. I am grateful to you for your tolerance of me and my shortcomings of youth, when I grumbled and rebelled against the change you made in our mode of living, from so much to so little.

"As a young child, I lived in your parents' home; your mother was a great and good woman; she trained me, taught me how to be a brave, courageous wife and how to keep the love and respect of her son, my future husband. As the years passed and you became India's most beloved leader, I had none of the fears that beset the wife who may be cast aside when her husband has climbed the ladder of success, as so often happens in other countries. I knew that death would still find us husband and wife.''[2]

I wonder whether another beautiful affirmed and affirming person of our time, Mother Teresa, had been inspired by Kasturbai to devote her life to the dying destitutes of Calcutta.

---

2. *Autobiography of a Yogi,* by Paramahansa Yogananda (Los Angeles: Self-Realization Fellowship, 1973) p. 506.

Addendum I

ON ASSERTION
AND
AGGRESSION

Most of the literature on aggression seems to be founded on the assumption that man is aggressive by nature, that is, according to Webster, "tending to, or characterized by a first or unprovoked attack, or act of hostility, the first act of injury leading to a war or controversy."

In my studies and personal clinical observations—corroborated by those of my colleague from the Netherlands, Anna A. Terruwe, M.D.—I have never found irrefutable proof that man, or for that matter, animal possesses an innate aggressive drive.

However, what has become clear without a shadow of a doubt, is that man has an innate assertive drive. Assertive, as Webster defines the term, means: 1) characterized by, or disposed to affirm, to declare with assurance, to state positively; 2) to maintain or defend, e.g. one's rights or prerogatives." This as-

sertive drive is also properly called the drive for self-preservation and self-realization (a term to be distinguished from self-fulfillment and self-affirmation!).

Man has this drive in common with the animal. Animals fight only to protect their offspring or their territory or to secure food when they are hungry. They do not fight in order to destroy, but only to determine who is the strongest. As soon as this has been determined the fighting stops.

Man, however, is capable of acquiring an aggressive bent. The man who is truly free can use his freedom of choice to attack others without provocation for the purpose of killing them, of capturing their possessions, of taking away their freedom, or to enslave them for the sake of satisfying his lust for power. But what man is truly free? The answer to this question is, of course, the fully affirmed man. And it is precisely he who is capable of abusing his freedom of choice—in contrast to the unaffirmed person—for the purpose of either affirming or denying others.

Seemingly unprovoked acts of aggression by an unaffirmed person, even when directed at strangers are in essence and in the strict sense of the word assertive acts prompted by his frustration, anger and hate of those who did not give him his due, who provoked him by depriving him of his fundamental need to experience himself as good and worthwhile. Having been denied his natural right to his second or *psychic birth* as I have described it in this book, he comes to hate those who deprived

him of this right. He may through his hate perform
an act of violence against these persons themselves,
or others who represent those who have denied him.

Virtually all research studies of murderers report
various degrees of denial in childhood or evidence
of its consequences, like brutalization by parents
or parent-surrogates, humiliation, loneliness, feelings
of worthlessness and self-negation, depression and
thoughts of suicide. Most murderers, the studies indicate, do not come from a climate of violence, but
rather from a climate of denial, from a milieu which
had denied them their psychic birth!

The distinction in motivation between the violent
acts of the unaffirmed and the affirmed persons to
which I have drawn attention here, has special significance for society's attempts at dealing with violence.

Neither one ever calls for the solution of prevention by conditioned training as advocated by
B. F. Skinner and others. The "aggression" of the
unaffirmed person can only be prevented through
affirmation.

Addendum II

AFFIRMATION
AND
HAPPINESS

One of the subtitles I considered for this book was: "The tragedy of non-affirmation, self-affirmation, and pseudo-affirmation." Another one could have been: "Affirmation—the key to human happiness." Both subtitles would have been pertinent and to the point. The truth of the former has been amply demonstrated in this book. In regard to the latter, I would like to ask: "Does the claim, that affirmation is the key to human happiness square with the truth as presented, for example, by such great lovers of the truth as Augustine, Aristotle, and Thomas Aquinas?"

Augustine wrote with striking simplicity in the fourth century, "Surpassingly happy is he who has everything he wants."[1]

---

1. Augustine, *De Trinitate*, 13, 5.

Eight centuries later Aquinas recast this sentence by saying, "He who has everything he wants is happy in that he has what he wants," only to add —in order to put the emphasis where it belongs— "which having however takes place by something other than an act of the will,[2]. . .that having takes place as cognition; cognition is having." In other words Aquinas holds that the essence of happiness consists in an act of the intellect! This becomes understandable when we realize that for Aquinas the intellect includes sense cognition and thus also feeling since elsewhere he says "man doesn't know the full truth until his feelings 'know' what his intellect knows." For example, a child may have been told repeatedly by his mother that the stove is hot, but the child will not know the full truth of what a hot stove is until he has felt it. And one of Aquinas' Spanish commentators, Bartolomé de Medina, restated his idea about human happiness equally succinctly, "the happy life does not mean loving what we possess, but possessing what we love"![3]

In this book I have defined "being affirmed" as having one's goodness revealed to one self by another." This means that in being affirmed we come to know, on the sense level as well as on the intellectual level, our own goodness. We "come to

---

2. *Summa Theologica* I, II, 3, 4, and 5.

3. In Ramirez, III, 176.

possess" in acts of sensory and intellectual cognition or knowing that we are good and worthwhile, valuable and lovable. Therefore, we possess our own lovable self, we possess what we love—and this, de Medina says, constitutes the happy life!

In other words we may indeed conclude that our claim is in full agreement with the great philosophers: affirmation is the key to human happiness. The affirming other, in making my own goodness known and felt by me, makes it possible for me to possess what I love, my lovable self (and much more, of course) and thus to be happy!

ACKNOWLEGDEMENTS

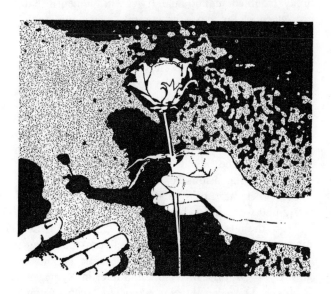

It is not generally realized, unfortunately, that the most adequate way of reciprocating a gift is the very reception of that gift. It is precisely this profound truth that gives meaning to my reception of the varied gifts from the persons who contributed, directly or indirectly, to the publication of this book.

From my colleague Dr. Anna A. Terruwe of Nymegen, Netherlands. During eighteen years of fascinating dialogue on both sides of the Atlantic Ocean she has taught me many things which, although ignored by and large in medical school and psychiatric training, are indispensable to every person entrusted with the well-being of emotionally and spiritually troubled individuals. It was in Nymegen that my *education* as a psychotherapist began and took over from where my *training* as a psychiatrist had left off. When my studies of man, the rational animal, were furthered by those of man, the spiritual human being created in the image of a loving God, I at last began to comprehend the how and why of many of his afflictions. To share some of Dr. Terruwe's novel ideas with others in this book is a source of deep satisfaction, equalled only by that derived from the new dimensions of my professional life. These dimensions replaced the disenchantment I had experienced prior to discovering and affirming this gifted woman psychiatrist.

From the late W.J.A.J. Duynstee, C.SS.R., LL.D., pioneer in the reapprochement between the monumental discoveries of Freud and authentic Thomistic anthropology. First in Rome, and later in Nymegen, Professor Duynstee introduced me to facets of philosophy and theology which revolutionized my concepts of man's beginning and end. His incontestable logic and masterful reasoning on the subject of man's free will, on the difference between "you must" and "you may", resolved for me forever the seemingly irreconcilable conflict between the suffering of man and divine love. His psychotheological interpretations, commencing with his 1935 lecture on "The Theory of Repression in the Light of Thomistic Psychology" have proven of immense practical value in my daily encounters with obsessive-compulsive neurotics.

From my many patients who, each in his own unique way, contributed patiently to the never ending process of my education in understanding man in his search for happiness and the various man-made psychological obstacles which keep him from possessing it fully.

From Roger Junak whom I was so fortunate to meet for the first time in his beautiful and moving self-portrait in oil, and who responded so generously to my request to provide the sketches for this book. The strokes of his pen masterfully succeeded in conveying feelings, moods and thoughts which my words failed to express fully.

From Walter J. Hanss, Jr., whose long dormant artistic talents came to life so beautifully in the stunning, almost mysterious reproduction of "The Prisoner" on the front jacket, in his photograph of the rose, the symbol of affirmation, and in the two other photographs he so graciously supplied.

From Helen D. Sweeney who patiently re-created the manuscript of this book from my hand-scribbled notes which normally only a pharmacist would be able to decipher. With the perspicacious mind of the born poet and teacher she tactfully, yet assertively convinced me of the need to improve here and there my grammar and style. Her rapid-fire typing provided the final touch to the birth of *Born Only Once.*

From Charles R. Grande whose studies of my writings and those of Anna Terruwe drove him well beyond the academic requirements for his M.A. in psychology and beyond the sagacity of many a psychologist with a string of degrees. His comprehension of aristotelian-thomistic psychology bodes well for his future success as a clinical psychologist.

From my wife and children who always let me be. Throughout the years they cheerfully shared the risks of promoting new and different ideas in the field of psychiatry, and of applying them in clinical endeavors of great promise, yet subject to the frailties of man. Their constant affirmation presents incontestable proof that genuine faith in another human being's goodness is the root source of unselfish love of self and others, of self-confidence and courage. It provides the staying power whenever one is faced with the question, "whether 'tis nobler in the mind to suffer the slings and arrows of outrageous fortune, or to take arms against a sea of troubles, and by opposing end them?"

From F.M., R.M., A.C., J.C.W., B.J.F., J.C.F., and others who supplied spiritual inspiration, counsel and support when the demands of new enterprises seemed overwhelming, or when trials and disillusionments put to the test the required response of faith and surrender.

And from the Giver of the first gift . . . in the beginning!

POSTSCRIPT

I consider it necessary to draw the reader's attention to the fact that not every treatment or counseling center with the word 'affirmation' in its title, nor every psychiatrist or psychologist claiming to provide affirmation therapy, can be assumed to practice this therapy correctly as described here and in our other publications. Not infrequently investigation of such claims will reveal little more than a combination of assertive training techniques and some probing type of psychotherapy. The serious danger of such approaches is, of course, that non–assertive deprivation neurotics are trained to become assertive, self–affirming persons, frequently in the image of the therapists and counselors who themselves are unaffirmed individuals.

It has come to my attention that in some parts of this country group sensitivity training sessions of the "touch, feel and sex" variety are being advertised and conducted under the name of "affirmation therapy." Needless to say that an affirmed and affirming therapist or group facilitator would never use such techniques, nor, for that matter, any other techniques. Authentic affirmation follows solely and primarily from a person's "being," not his "doing"! One can only wonder to what extent the emergence of such harmful pseudo-affirmation centers, etc. is the result of such ill–defined talk about the healing touch of affirmation; self–affirmation is essential to human development, and the like.

In recent years some publications on the subject of affirmation have been circulated or published in book form which may well constitute plagiarism considering that a full and extensive discussion on this subject, together with a full description of the deprivation neurosis, originated with its discoverer, Anna A. Terruwe, M.D. Persons making contrary claims, or those failing to make proper and accurate reference in their writings to the publications of Dr. Terruwe and myself, are, if not willfully remiss, either confusing the maternal deprivation syndrome with that of the deprivation neurosis, or have failed to make a thorough study of the world psychiatric literature.

The original description of the deprivation or frustration neurosis may be found in *The Neurosis in the Light of Rational Psychology* by A.A.A. Terruwe, M.D., translated by C.W. Baars, M.D., P.J. Kenedy & Sons, New York, 1960, and in *De Frustratie Neurose* by Dr. A.A.A. Terruwe, M.D., J.J. Romen & Zonen, Roermond en Maaseik, 1962. A few of the many books by Dr. Terruwe on various aspects of affirmation and self–affirmation are: *De Liefde Bouwt een Woning*, J.J. Romen & Zonen, 1967; *The Abode of Love*, Abbey Press, 1970; *Geloven zonder Angst en Vrees*, J.J. Romen & Zonen, 1971; *Geef My Je Hand*, De Tydstroom, 1972. Also, *The Significance of the Work of Dr. A.A.A. Terruwe for Psychiatry*, by Prof. Dr. J.J.G. Prick, De Tydstroom, 1973 (available only in Dutch).